FREE TO BE FRUITFUL

BIBLICAL FOUNDATIONS FOR HEALING AND FREEDOM

JOEY BENAMI

WESTBOW
PRESS
A DIVISION OF THOMAS NELSON

Scripture quotations taken from the New American Standard Bible®, Copyright © 1960, 1962, 1963, 1968, 1971, 1972, 1973, 1975, 1977, 1995 by The Lockman Foundation Used by permission." (www.Lockman.org)

WestBow Press books may be ordered through booksellers or by contacting:

WestBow Press
A Division of Thomas Nelson
1663 Liberty Drive
Bloomington, IN 47403
www.westbowpress.com
1-(866) 928-1240

Because of the dynamic nature of the Internet, any web addresses or links contained in this book may have changed since publication and may no longer be valid. The views expressed in this work are solely those of the author and do not necessarily reflect the views of the publisher, and the publisher hereby disclaims any responsibility for them.

Any people depicted in stock imagery provided by Thinkstock are models, and such images are being used for illustrative purposes only.

Author photo courtesy of J LeFlore Photography

Certain stock imagery © Thinkstock.

ISBN: 978-1-4497-3845-7 (sc)
ISBN: 978-1-4497-3844-0 (hc)
ISBN: 978-1-4497-3846-4 (e)
Library of Congress Control Number: 2012901207

Printed in the United States of America

WestBow Press rev. date: 03/26/2012

INTRODUCTION

HOW TO READ THIS BOOK

I wrote this book for you, the reader, and I'd like to tell you how to get the most out of it.

First, read and re-read slowly! Every statement in this book was well thought-out. Every sentence and every word were crafted carefully and they are packed with purpose.

Second, read every passage of Scripture. I have tried to limit what I say to explain and illustrate the Scriptures I'm sharing with you. I have provided almost every Bible passage for you within the book so you have all you need right here. Much of what I bring out comes from subtle meanings lost in our English translations but present in the original words, grammar and composition.

Finally, hear what the Spirit is communicating to you as you read. Pause frequently if necessary and ask Him, "Father, what lies have I believed about what I'm reading?" Repent from agreeing with whatever lie He shows you. Then ask Him, "Father, what is the truth you want me to believe now?" Transformation takes place when God reveals the lies you may have believed and tells you the truth about Himself, His love and acceptance; about yourself, your value and worth; and about any circumstance in your experience.

PART I

FRUITFULNESS

CHAPTER ONE

LAND

When God wanted to communicate to us, He chose to do it through words. God uses words to tell us about the things He created. The words He uses to talk about physical realities are the same He uses to talk about spiritual realities. In Scripture, the first mentions of a word give shape to its meaning. Those early mentions are also foundational for understanding the spiritual realities behind it.

A very important term in Scripture is the word translated earth in Genesis 1. In Hebrew the word is "eretz." This word is first mentioned in the opening verse of the Bible: "In the beginning God created the heavens and the earth" (Gen 1:1).

This verse introduces God's focus on the land. God's intention was creating a fruitful land that would sustain life. The land would feed many people with its fruitfulness. God is all about life, and He established that physical life would be sustained primarily through food. There are two central reasons why the land is the focus of Genesis 1.

THE LAND IS ISRAEL

The people of Israel, the original readers of Genesis 1, fresh out of Egypt and on their way to Canaan, would have understood this

3

chapter in a very specific way. "Eretz," translated "earth" or "land," is the primary designation for the land of Canaan. The Divine author here, God Himself, is hinting at the reader. Yes, there's a sense in which "eretz" in Genesis 1 means the entire earth. However, the reader is also supposed to understand it as *the* land, the land of Israel. Genesis 1 talks about the creation of the land promised to Israel, the land toward which they were going in order to possess it. Just as the account of creation leaves out details of the vast universe, so the same account focuses on one piece of land out of the whole earth.

This revelation opens up dynamic potentials in our understanding and prophetic applications of this passage. These potentials have always been there in the text. The Holy Spirit holds them in His hand. He unveils our eyes enabling us to see.

One prophetic pattern that comes from understanding Genesis 1 as the land of Israel is the garden as a temple. Genesis 2:8 says: "The LORD God planted a garden toward the east, in Eden." Notice that the garden is "in" Eden, on the east part of Eden. The garden had a river and in its midst it had the tree of life. That garden was a copy of the real garden in heaven.

> Rev 22:1-2 Then he showed me a river of the water of life, clear as crystal, coming from the throne of God and of the Lamb, in the middle of its street. On either side of the river was the tree of life.

When the new heavens and new earth are introduced, notice that what we get is Jerusalem.

> Rev 21:1-3 Then I saw a new heaven and a new earth; for the first heaven and the first earth passed

away, and there is no longer any sea. And I saw the holy city, new Jerusalem, coming down out of heaven from God, made ready as a bride adorned for her husband. And I heard a loud voice from the throne, saying, "Behold, the tabernacle of God is among men, and He will dwell among them, and they shall be His people, and God Himself will be among them.

This is similar to what I am proposing here. The focus of Genesis 1 is on the land of Israel. The garden-temple was located in that land, in none other than what later came to be known as Jerusalem.

Rev 21:22 I saw no temple in it [in the city], for the Lord God the Almighty and the Lamb are its temple.

The river comes from the very throne of God, and the throne of God is in the holy of holies! The garden of Eden, in Eden, was a temple. God's throne was there, dwelling with Adam and Eve. The river was there and the tree of life was there. Eden is the city of Jerusalem, and inside of it, to the east of it, was the temple, the garden.[1] The land which Genesis 1 and 2 talk about is "eretz Yisrael," the land of Israel.

YOU ARE THE LAND

The second reason why the land is the focus of Genesis 1 is that you and I are the land. In Matthew 13, the Lord Jesus said,

"When anyone hears the word of the kingdom and does not understand it, the evil one comes and

---

[1]   And just as the garden was to the east of Eden, so the temple mount today is in east Jerusalem. Even the entrance to the tabernacle and the temple looked to the east.

snatches away what has been sown in his heart. This is the one on whom seed was sown beside the road.[2]

The soil, the land, is you and me. This fact gives God an amazing range of meanings to communicate truth to us and about us.

The ways in which Genesis 1 focuses on the land carry great significance for us. Let's examine that significance in the following three areas.

1. Creation
This focus emphasizes the fruitfulness for which God designed us. Just as the land was made fruitful in order to sustain life, to feed others, so we are viewed as fruitful land because "The lips of the righteous feed many."[3] It is God's desire to make a Joseph out of us, each in his or her unique way, so He can feed the world through our fruitfulness.

2. Israel
Once our eyes are unveiled to see the land of Israel in Genesis 1, the prophetic applications rush to the mind. As land, you and I aren't just any land. The truths about the land of Israel are prophetic patterns about us.[4]

The Holy Land
As land, you are holy in Him and are being sanctified and cleansed from the defilement of the "Canaanites," and anointed by the touch of His presence as His temple.

---

[2] Matt 13:19
[3] Prov 10:21
[4] This isn't saying that the church replaces Israel and the Jewish people in the Bible; it only speaks of the application of Scripture.

The Promised Land

You as land have your origin and your hope in a promise. You are the son of a promise as Isaac was, born through faith on a promise that defies impossibility. And because of that promise, you act as the heir of that land. You still wait to see that promise realized, the land of your soul totally under the possession of your new nature.

The Covenant Land

You as land are a covenant land. As such, you are made fruitful (covenant with Adam); you have received a promise not be flooded again (covenant with Noah); you are a city with better foundations (Abrahamic covenant); you are blessed for your obedience (Mosaic covenant); you will have an anointed king over you forever (Davidic covenant); and you will be made new (new covenant).

The Inherited Land

You as inherited land are God's own inheritance and portion. You are the land where He chose to make His dwelling. You are His and He is jealous over Zion, over you.

The Conquered Land

You as conquered land are meant to live in prosperity and rest from your enemies. The spiritual war fought over you has been won. God will bring, progressively more of your territory (your soul) under your possession.

3. Garden

We are the temple of God through the Holy Spirit, both corporately and individually. That metaphor has built-in a great amount of revelation about us. In the garden of Eden, we have a foretaste of all that God's heavenly temple is: God dwelling with man as sole source of life and truth, and man worshiping God and keeping His word. That's exactly what our reality is as God's temple.

Two other revelatory metaphors that are present in the garden, and in us, are the river and the trees. The prophet Ezekiel says:

Then he brought me back to the door of the house [the temple]; and behold, water was flowing from under the threshold of the house toward the east, for the house faced east.[5]

Verse 6-9,

He said to me, "Son of man, have you seen this?" Then he brought me back to the bank of the river. Now when I had returned, behold, on the bank of the river there were very many trees on the one side and on the other. Then he said to me, "These waters go out toward the eastern region and go down into the Arabah; then they go toward the sea, being made to flow into the sea, and the waters of the sea become fresh. "It will come about that every living creature which swarms in every place where the river goes, will live. And there will be very many fish, for these waters go there and the others become fresh; so everything will live where the river goes.

The waters going to the Arabah means they go east to the Jordan River from the temple, and then flow south. They flow to the Dead Sea. The Hebrew word for "fresh" is "rapha" which means "healed." "Everything will live where the river goes." The Dead Sea is dead no more! It is healed! It is now capable of sustaining life.

Verse 12,

"By the river on its bank, on one side and on the other, will grow all kinds of trees for food. Their leaves will not wither and their fruit will not fail. They will bear every month because their water

---

[5]   Ezek 47:1

flows from the sanctuary, and their fruit will be for
food and their leaves for healing."

These are Eden-like conditions during the Millennium. Both, Eden
and the Millennium, are foretastes of the world to come, the eternal
temple described in Revelation 22. And this is also true about us as
garden. The river that flows from us when we're filled with the Spirit
brings healing to others. The fruit from us as trees feed many, and
even the leaves from our lives are for the healing of nations! We were
designed to be a fruitful land indeed!

CHAPTER TWO

AGRICULTURE

AGRICULTURE AND CREATION

The world of agriculture is the Bible's premier metaphor. To focus on the land is to focus on its agriculture. Of the abundance of metaphors found in the Bible, agriculture is second to none. Therefore, to say that you are land is to make a declaration rich in a variety of meanings and applications.

The content of Genesis 1, the things created each day, show a focus on agriculture. The land benefits directly from the creation of light, the appearing of dry land and the creation of sun, moon and stars with all their cycles. These benefits come in the form of agriculture.

We have talked about the first mention in Scripture of the word "eretz," "land." Now let's talk about the following six occurrences. I will highlight them for you.

In order to prepare the land for agriculture, God removed the water that was covering the earth, "drowning" fruitfulness, so to speak.

Gen 1:10 God called the dry land **earth**, and the gathering of the waters He called seas; and God saw that it was good.[6]

Once the water was removed God gave a creative command:

Gen 1:11-12 Then God said, "Let the **earth** sprout vegetation, plants yielding seed, and fruit trees on the **earth** bearing fruit after their kind with seed in them"; and it was so. The **earth** brought forth vegetation, plants yielding seed after their kind, and trees bearing fruit with seed in them, after their kind; and God saw that it was good.[7]

God's creative command started agriculture, made the land fruitful. All that was left to do now was to ensure that agriculture could continue. To that end He created the light that would feed life to the land, fueling its fruitfulness. Speaking of sun, moon and stars, God said:

Gen 1:15 "Let them be for lights in the expanse of the heavens to give light on the **earth**"; and it was so.[8]

Gen 1:17 God placed them in the expanse of the heavens to give light on the **earth**.[9]

The sun relates to agriculture not only providing light and heat, but also determining the yearly agricultural calendar in the land of Israel. That includes the rainy seasons. The moon also relates to the calendar and together sun and moon determine the times, not only in days, weeks and years, so important for Israel's Sabbath and cycles

---

[6]   Emphasis added.
[7]   Emphasis added.
[8]   Emphasis added.
[9]   Emphasis added.

of seven years and 49 years, but also for the appointed times of God's feasts. In these annual feasts Israel would appear before God with the first fruits and the tithes of their agriculture.

But the land is not an end in itself. All this was God's way to provide for man, the crown of His creation.

Here are some patterns we see. God prepares you as land by removing whatever is "drowning" your fruitfulness. God's infinite creativity and commanding power have one focus: making you fruitful as land. Your fruitfulness is a process that follows a cycle, illustrated in Israel's yearly agricultural cycle. And finally, the purpose of your fruitfulness is to sustain others with life.

AGRICULTURE AND WORSHIP

Imagine the fruitfulness of the ground before the fall of man, before the ground was cursed due to sin. Before it grew "thorns and thistles." Most of us understand that Adam had a job in the garden, an agricultural job. But think for a moment, what was there for him to do? I mean, no bugs to kill, no watering to get done, no weeds to uproot. The vines didn't need to be prune. Adam and Eve just had to extend their hand, pluck the fruit and eat!

We already established that the garden in Eden was a temple. I think you would agree that Adam and Eve were priests. Remember the priests later in the Torah? They didn't work the land. In fact, they didn't even inherit land in Israel for them to farm. The tithes were their portion and inheritance. The priests' work was to be temple work. Not only would they offer sacrifices but also teach people the Torah and act as judges. Why would Adam and Eve, God's original priests, have agricultural jobs? It doesn't make sense. Look at them in the garden.

> Gen 2:15 Then the LORD God took the man and
> put him into the garden of Eden to cultivate it and
> keep it.

First, let's see how the Hebrew word translated "put" is used elsewhere. I will highlight the English word that translates our target Hebrew word.

> Ex 16:33-34 Moses said to Aaron, "Take a jar and
> put an omerful of manna in it, and **place** it before
> the LORD to be kept throughout your generations."
> As the LORD commanded Moses, so Aaron **placed**
> it before the Testimony, to be kept.[10]

> Deut 12:10 "When you cross the Jordan and live in
> the land which the LORD your God is giving you to
> inherit, and He gives you **rest** from all your enemies
> around you so that you live in security . . ."[11]

The verb translated "put" can be used of objects "placed," like the manna, in the holy of holies, the very presence of God. It also speaks of Israel in the land at "rest" under God's protection from her enemies. I suggest here that Adam and Eve enjoyed the same in the garden, their "temple." They were protected in God's "rest" from the enemy, possessing their own land. They were also "put" in God's very presence as holy priests. All this corroborates what we are about to learn.[12]

Paraphrasing Genesis 2:15, "Adam was put in the garden as a priest to 'avad' and 'shamar.'" From the Hebrew word "avad" derive two other Hebrew words: "abodah," which is one of the biblical words

---

[10] Emphasis added.
[11] Emphasis added.
[12] I am indebted to John H. Sailhamer, *Genesis*, ed. Frank E. Gaebelein and J. D. Douglas, vol. 2 of Expositor's Bible Commentary. Accordance electronic ed. (Grand Rapids: Zondervan, 1990), n.p.

used for "worship," and the word "ebed" translated "slave," and "servant."

Let's look more in detail. After Adam sinned "The LORD God sent him out from the garden of Eden, to **cultivate** (avad) the ground from which he was taken."[13] And after Cain murdered Abel, God said to him in punishment "When you **cultivate** (avad) the ground, it will no longer yield its strength to you . . ."[14] God announced to Abraham that his descendants "Will be **enslaved** (avad) and oppressed four hundred years"[15] in the land of Egypt. God said to Moses: "When you have brought the people out of Egypt, you shall **worship** (avad) God at this mountain."[16]

The consequence of Adam and Cain's actions was "enslavement" to the ground, servitude to it. In both verses the Hebrew word for ground is "adamah," from which we get "Adam." It's an ironic reversal. Adam, who rose from the "adamah," will now serve (be enslaved to), the "adamah," the ground.

Putting all this together the evidence mounts in favor of Adam and Eve "put" in the Garden as priests "to worship," not to serve, cultivate or be enslaved to the ground. "Cultivate the ground" would be the result of the fall (Genesis 3:17-19), but Genesis 2:15 is before the fall. Of these two uses of the root word "avad," the one that fits best the pre-fall context is "worship."

The other word used in Genesis 2:15 completes this beautiful picture. The Hebrew word "shamar" is the term used most frequently to "keep" or "guard" the word of God. Let's see two sample passages:

> Gen 18:19 For I [God] have chosen him [Abraham],
> so that he may command his children and his

---

13   Gen 3:23. Emphasis added.
14   Gen 4:12. Emphasis added.
15   Gen 15:13. Emphasis added.c
16   Ex 3:12. Emphasis added.

household after him to **keep** the way of the LORD by doing righteousness and justice . . . [17]

Gen 26:5 Because Abraham obeyed Me and **kept** My charge, My commandments, My statutes and My laws.[18]

The beautiful picture of Adam and Eve in the garden is that of God's priests, "put" there by God so they can "worship" Him and "keep" His commands. They were in a garden-temple, blessed with fruitfulness and the sustenance of food, in a land greatly fertile and made good by God for their provision. They were there to worship God in profound adoration, and to obey His word in great reverence. That's the picture of blessedness, of fruitfulness, that God desires to paint for us as well!

AGRICULTURE AND RAIN

Noah's name in Hebrew is "Noach," and his name is related to the word translated "rest" (nacham) in Genesis 5:29:

Now he called his name **Noah**, saying, "This one will give us **rest** (nacham) from our work and from the toil of our hands arising from the ground which the LORD has cursed.[19]

The play on words and meaning is evident. However, what's not so evident is how that "rest" ever happened. Noah is known for the ark and the flood, and he's known for the rainbow, but the prophecy over his life implied in his name had to do with rain. The rain brought "an ease," a rest from the difficulties of agriculture, diminishing the effects of the curse. The rain made agriculture easier, easing up the

---

17 Emphasis added.
18 Emphasis added.
19 Emphasis added.

effects of the curse in Genesis 3 for the whole world.[20] This meant a more fruitful agriculture. The more fruitful your agriculture is as land, the less of a slave you are. Spiritual freedom is directly related to how fruitful you are!

---

[20] Scripture has much to say about the meaning and the significance of rain, so we will return to that theme later in this book.

CHAPTER THREE

BLESSING

Having established that Genesis 1 focuses on the land, and that this focus has to do with agriculture, with a fruitful land, let's see now the relationship between God's blessing and fruitfulness.

GOODNESS

In preparation for His blessing, God made sure that the land, and all He created for its fruitfulness, was good. God "saw" that all He had made was "good." That is repeated in all but one of the days of creation. What is the meaning of the word "good"? And even further, what can we say about the activity of "seeing"?

The Hebrew word "raah," translated "saw" or "see," is of great importance in Scripture. So is the activity of "seeing." The sentence "God saw . . ." is repeated 7 times in Genesis 1. That should tell us about its importance and significance in this chapter. In Genesis 2:19 God brings the animals He created for Adam to "see" what he would call them. God left it to Adam to decide. A chapter later, in Genesis 3:6, Eve "saw" that the tree was good for food. The difference between these two instances of "seeing" is that God had delegated to Adam the decision to "see," but Eve took it upon herself to decide, to "see" what was good for her. God had already decided what was good for food, but Eve was deceived and went against that. It is clear from this example that the activity of "seeing" means to evaluate and make a decision about something, considering it good or not.

The same dynamic occurred with Abraham and Lot. Genesis 13:10 says that "Lot lifted up his eyes and saw all the valley of the Jordan, that it was well watered." But God told Abraham in 13:14, "Lift up your eyes and look . . ." Lot, deciding that watered land was good for him, chose Sodom and Gomorrah. These cities were located outside the land of Israel, the blessed land. But God chose for Abraham the fruitful land of Israel. In Scripture, when the activity of "seeing" is theologically important, it is reserved for God. When man "sees," disaster usually follows.

In Genesis 22:8 Abraham said, "God will provide for Himself the lamb." Through the activity of "seeing" God not only evaluates and decides what is good, He also provides what is good. The word translated "provide" in this verse is the same Hebrew word "raah" translated "see." God "will see to it" that a lamb is provided.

> Gen 22:14 Abraham called the name of that place
> The LORD Will Provide, as it is said to this day, "In
> the mount of the LORD it will be provided."

"Seeing" is the activity of God by which He evaluates and decides what is good and evil, and provides what is good. What we have in Genesis 1 is that God not only evaluates and determines as good what He has created, but He Himself provides what is good, He sees to it that good is provided.

This brings us to the question of what is "good." We mentioned that in every day of creation, except one, God "saw that it was good." On the second day, when He made the expanse and divided the waters, the report of that being good is lacking. How come? The reason is that no progress was made toward God's goal of making the land fruitful. Part of the water that covered the land was removed, but water still covered the land. Something is good if it is decided as such by God, if it benefits or advances His purpose. Something is good when it is beneficial for God's purpose. His purpose in Genesis 1 was to make the land fruitful. God knows and decides what is beneficial to promote fruitfulness, and He provides that. Good is that which is beneficial for fruitfulness.

Why focus on fruitfulness? Because fruitfulness is at the very heart of God's blessing. Fruitfulness is the way God provides food, sustenance.

BLESSING

After God created Adam and Eve in His image and likeness, He blessed them. The Bible says:

> Gen 1:28 God blessed them; and God said to them, "Be fruitful and multiply . . ."

Most Bible interpreters take the imperatives "Be fruitful and multiply" as commands to Adam and Eve. In other words, they read it as if the text said, "God blessed them. And after He was done blessing them, He commanded them to be fruitful and multiply." But that's not the best way to read this passage. The commands here are imperatives of promise.[21] Fruitfulness is God's assurance to us. He commands fruitfulness over us and it will happen, just like He commanded light and it came to be. God commanded fruitfulness and multiplication over Adam and Eve. He didn't command Adam and Eve to be fruitful and multiply because it was impossible for them to do that for themselves. What God said to Adam and Eve is the very content of His blessing. In other words, we should read it

---

[21] These commands "...express a distinct assurance... or promise... especially in commands, the fulfillment of which is altogether out of the power of the person addressed." "Gesenius' Hebrew Grammar/110. The Imperative," *Wikisource, The Free Library,* //en.wikisource. org/w/index.php?title=Gesenius%27_Hebrew_Grammar/110._The_ Imperative&oldid=2186076 (accessed January 4, 2012).

as, "God blessed them by saying, 'Be fruitful and multiply . . .'" We can corroborate throughout Genesis that God takes upon Himself the responsibility of making people fruitful. Notice that fruitfulness is always a manifestation of blessing.

> Gen 12:2 And I will make you a great nation, and I will bless you.

> Gen 17:20 As for Ishmael . . . I will bless him, and will make him fruitful and will multiply him exceedingly . . .

> Gen 22:17 Indeed I will greatly bless you, and I will greatly multiply your seed . . .

> Gen 26:24 The LORD appeared to him the same night and said, "I am the God of your father Abraham; Do not fear, for I am with you. I will bless you, and multiply your descendants . . ."

> Gen 28:3 May God Almighty bless you and make you fruitful and multiply you . . .

The way God blessed Adam and Eve was by pronouncing them fruitful. But he didn't stop in verse 28. Verse 29 continued the blessing and verse 30 extended it even to all the animals.

> Gen 1:29-30 Then God said, "Behold, I have given you every plant yielding seed that is on the surface of all the earth, and every tree which has fruit yielding seed; it shall be food for you; and to every beast of the earth and to every bird of the sky and to every thing that moves on the earth which has life, I have given every green plant for food"; and it was so.

Part of the blessing of God was abundant provision of food, sustenance. Look at a key passage were God's blessing is tied to provision.

> Gen 27:27-28 So he [Isaac] came close and kissed him [Jacob disguised as Esau]; and when he smelled the smell of his garments, he blessed him and said, "See, the smell of my son is like the smell of a field which the LORD has blessed; Now may God give you of the dew of heaven, and of the fatness of the earth, and an abundance of grain and new wine.

Notice that Isaac's blessing provided Jacob with rain (the dew of heaven), oil (the fatness from olives), abundant grain (primarily barley and wheat) and wine (the fruit of vineyards). These were the main products of the land of Israel.

But we know the story doesn't end there. Esau came to be blessed and found that Jacob had deceived Isaac and received the blessing. Esau asked a penetrating question.

> Gen 27:36-38 And he [Esau] said, "Have you not reserved a blessing for me?" But Isaac replied to Esau, "Behold . . . with grain and new wine I have sustained him [Jacob]. Now as for you then, what can I do, my son?" Esau said to his father, "Do you have only one blessing, my father?

What a difficult question this was for Isaac! His answer really was "Yes, my son, I have only one blessing."

> Gen 27:39 Then Isaac his father answered and said to him, "Behold, away from the fertility of the earth shall be your dwelling, and away from the dew of heaven from above."

Jacob got *the* blessing, the one and only! The only blessing Isaac ever had and the only blessing there ever was. The blessing Abraham gave Isaac. The blessing God gave Noah. The blessing God gave Adam and Eve. There was only one blessing. The blessing of Genesis 1 is it! And don't miss the fact that this blessing was really part of a covenant. God's blessing is at the heart of His covenant with His people. Through His blessing God makes His people fruitful and provides for them abundantly. Isaac could not give Esau "the fertility of the land" or "the dew of heaven." Can you see the centrality of rain and fruitfulness, food provision, to God's covenant and blessing?

Food, that is, bread and meat, stand for the word. It stands for Jesus Himself. Every word from God is sustenance. God wants to give us His word, He wants to speak to us and give us words. But not just a little of it. He wants to give us crops, entire harvests of it, well-developed teachings. He wants to give us the barley, the wheat, the olives and the grapes; year round crops. A harvest in every season, year after year!

Covenant

The centrality of agriculture in God's blessing and covenant is dramatically portrayed in Isaac's blessing over Jacob and his inability to bless Esau. Notice now Jacob's beautiful blessing over Joseph,

> Gen 49:22 Joseph is a fruitful bough, a fruitful bough by a spring; its branches [a vine] run over a wall.

> Gen 49:25 From the God of your father who helps you, and by the Almighty who blesses you with blessings of heaven above [rain], blessings of the deep that lies beneath [land], blessings of the breasts and of the womb [human and animals].

The blessing of Abraham and Isaac went to Jacob, and from him to all his sons, not just one of them, but to the entire nation:

> Lev 26:3-5 If you walk in My statutes and keep My commandments so as to carry them out, then I shall give you rains in their season, so that the land will yield its produce and the trees of the field will bear their fruit. Indeed, your threshing will last for you until grape gathering, and grape gathering will last until sowing time. You will thus eat your food to the full and live securely in your land.

The covenant promise to Israel as a nation was that walking with God would bring fruitful agriculture, both, physical and spiritual.

CURSE

The reverse is also true. Unfaithfulness to the covenant brings unfruitfulness. We see this with Adam right from the start. The ground was cursed on account of his sin. Cain made matters even worse for himself:

> Gen 4:10-12 He [God] said, "What have you done? The voice of your brother's blood is crying to Me from the ground. "Now you are cursed from the ground, which has opened its mouth to receive your brother's blood from your hand. "When you cultivate the ground, it will no longer yield its strength to you; you will be a vagrant and a wanderer on the earth."

We see the same at the corporate level with Israel.

> Lev 26:17-20 'I will set My face against you so that you will be struck down before your enemies; and those who hate you will rule over you, and you will

flee when no one is pursuing you. 'If also after these things you do not obey Me, then I will punish you seven times more for your sins. 'I will also break down your pride of power; I will also make your sky like iron and your earth like bronze. 'Your strength will be spent uselessly, for your land will not yield its produce and the trees of the land will not yield their fruit.

Notice the progression in the following passage.

Deut 11:13-17 "It shall come about, if you listen obediently to my commandments which I am commanding you today, to love the LORD your God and to serve Him with all your heart and all your soul, that He will give the rain for your land in its season, the early and late rain, that you may gather in your grain and your new wine and your oil. "He will give grass in your fields for your cattle, and you will eat and be satisfied. "Beware that your hearts are not deceived, and that you do not turn away and serve other gods and worship them. "Or the anger of the LORD will be kindled against you, and He will shut up the heavens so that there will be no rain and the ground will not yield its fruit; and you will perish quickly from the good land which the LORD is giving you.

The very first component of God's blessing is the rain. We saw that with Isaac's blessing of Jacob and we see it in these two passages from Leviticus and Deuteronomy.

OBSTACLES
In the parable of the sower in Matthew 13, three out of four soils, representing people, are unfruitful. One soil is hard, another is

rocky and the third is full of thorns and thistles. We can look in Scripture and in the natural world, and find applications from these conditions. However, I have found that the farther back we go in Scripture the more ultimate answers we find. The ultimate revelation about the obstacles to fruitfulness is found in the first mention of those obstacles. Let's turn to Genesis 1:2 for ultimate answers about our lack of fruitfulness.

CHAPTER FOUR

OBSTACLES

WHAT ARE THE OBSTACLES?

Genesis 1:2 says,

> The earth was formless and void, and darkness was
> over the surface of the deep, and the Spirit of God
> was moving over the surface of the waters.

The words "formless" and "void" are translations of the Hebrew words "tohu" and "vohu" respectively. Rather than telling you what I think they mean, or giving you some unproven dictionary definitions for these words, let's use the best rule of interpretation: Scripture interprets Scripture. Let's find other passages that use these words, study their context and then with that evidence state what these words mean.

The prophet Jeremiah describes the devastation that came over the land because of the Babylonian invasion and exile. The Holy Spirit led Jeremiah to describe this devastation in the words of Genesis 1.

> I looked on the earth (eretz), and behold, it was
> **formless** (tohu) and **void** (vohu); and to the
> heavens, and they had no light. I looked on the

mountains, and behold, they were quaking, and all
the hills moved to and fro. I looked, and behold,
there was no man, and all the birds of the heavens
had fled. I looked, and behold, the fruitful land
was a wilderness, and all its cities were pulled down
before the LORD, before His fierce anger.[22]

Jeremiah speaks of the judgment over Israel for her unfaithfulness
to her covenant God. We know some of the things such judgment
implies: lack of rain (drought), and crop failures (famine). In short,
the judgment is a severe unfruitfulness. The severe unfruitfulness
experienced by Adam was a reversal to the unfruitfulness of the land.
In the same way, Jeremiah's description presents a judgment in terms
of an ironic reversal to the condition of unfruitfulness of the land
before God made it "good."

Notice that Jeremiah's focus is on the land. He sees it in an ironic
reversal returning back to an unfruitful state. The comparison is to
Genesis 1:2, with the land formless and void. Darkness covers the
land since there are no lights in the heavens. In absence of the waters
that covered the mountaintops, Jeremiah saw the mountains and
hills shaking. The image substitutes the waters that used to cover the
land. And just as it was in day one of the creation week, there was
no man and no animals. The heavens were empty and the land was
empty as well. Void. "The fruitful land was a wilderness."

Since God had promised never again to flood the earth, He carried
out His judgment after the flood by turning the land into an
unfruitful wilderness. The waters of Genesis 1 prevented the land
from being fruitful. After the flood, God uses the wilderness to
accomplish the same.

We could say that the emptiness, the absence of man and animals,
refers to "void," uninhabited. And on the other hand, the darkness

---

[22] Jer 4:23-26. Emphasis added.

and water, and in this case the wilderness, refers to "formless." But let's look at another key passage to see if these are sound conclusions.

Isaiah, likewise, uses the word "formless" in the context of the Babylonian exile:

> For thus says the LORD, who created the heavens (He is the God who formed the earth and made it, He established it and did not create it a **waste place** (tohu, "formless"), but formed it to be **inhabited** ("not void"), "I am the LORD, and there is none else.[23]

According to Isaiah, God didn't create the land for it to be a wilderness, an unfruitful waste place. In other words, He didn't create it for it to be formless. Because of that, He formed it. And He formed it for it to be inhabited, not void.

So we have that formless means unfruitful, and void means uninhabited. We can say then that in Genesis 1:2 the land was unfruitful and uninhabited. When the land is formless it is covered in darkness and flood, it is a wilderness, unfruitful.

Returning to chapter 1 of Genesis, these two words, formless (tohu) and void (vohu) give a natural outline of the chapter. Roughly, in the first 3 days God forms the land and in the second 3 days God fills the land.

By context, formless means the land is in darkness and covered by water, therefore unfruitful. Void means the land is empty of animals and people; therefore uninhabited.

The obstacles to our fruitfulness as land are also darkness and flood.

---

[23] Is 45:18. Emphasis added.

WHO REMOVES THE OBSTACLES?

Notice that the Trinity is involved in the removal of the obstacles. In the middle of darkness and flood,

> The Spirit of God was moving over the surface of the waters.[24]

The Hebrew word for Spirit is "ruach," and it means wind, spirit. We will tap into those meanings later on. The Holy Spirit was moving. The Hebrew word translated "moving" gives a picture of a mother bird hovering over her young in protective care.

> Deut 32:11 Like an eagle that stirs up its nest, that **hovers** over its young, He [God] spread His wings and caught them, He carried them on His pinions.[25]

This word paints a picture of the Spirit's tender, motherly care over the land, even as the earth was under water and in darkness. The Holy Spirit waited in readiness to remove the obstacles to fruitfulness.

The Father spoke. He issued a command of creativity and execution, bringing to pass His desire and decree.

What God spoke was a word. The Word, Yeshua Messiah, Jesus the Anointed One, created all things in the beginning. God created through the Word. Fruitfulness is God's desire, He commands it, He has design it and He brings it to pass. It is brought about through the Word and by the Spirit. It becomes words because fruitfulness is bread, and it becomes a river of water that flows from one's inner being, as Jesus said speaking of the Spirit.[26]

---

[24] Gen 1:2
[25] Emphasis added.
[26] John 7:38-39

How Are the Obstacles Removed?

The obstacles to fruitfulness, darkness and flood, are removed by separation.

> Gen 1:4 God separated the light from the darkness.

> Gen 1:6 Let it separate the waters from the waters.

> Gen 1:9 Let the waters below the heavens be gathered into one place, and let the dry land appear.

Let's look now in detail how this separation, how this removal, takes place.

CHAPTER FIVE

DARKNESS

WHAT IS DARKNESS?

The first obstacle God removes is darkness. This is a pattern because that's the order He always follows. But what does darkness stand for? In the natural, darkness epitomizes death, absence of life. Life can't grow and thrive in darkness. In agriculture, darkness is incapable of giving life and producing fruitfulness.

Darkness stands for spiritual blindness, the inability to see God and His activities; to discern, choose and know (experience) truth. Darkness stands for spiritual death for the unbeliever, and slumbering for the believer.

God addressed darkness first. How did He do it? He created light.

In a passage full of intentionality and purpose as Genesis 1, we should expect priority to carry elevated significance. Because God's creative week is a pattern that teaches us how He makes the land fruitful, we learn through it how He makes us fruitful and how He removes the obstacles to our fruitfulness. We learn how He does that to everybody, to us and the people to whom we minister.

HOW DOES LIGHT REMOVE DARKNESS?

We see in Genesis 1 the priority of light. Why? Because . . .

Light stands for life

> John 1:4 In Him was life, and the life was the Light of men.

Light stands for love

> 1 John 2:9-10 The one who says he is in the Light and yet hates his brother is in the darkness until now. The one who loves his brother abides in the Light and there is no cause for stumbling in him.

Light stands for revelation

> John 1:9 There was the true Light which, coming into the world, enlightens every man.

Watch these two statements now:

In order for God to make the land fruitful He removed darkness, creating life-giving light, which is a revelation of His love manifested in the sun.

In order for God to make people fruitful He removes their death and blindness, giving them a life-giving revelation of His love manifested in His Son.

> 2 Cor 4:4, 6 The god of this world has blinded the minds of the unbelieving so that they might not see the light of the gospel of the glory of Christ, who is the image of God . . . For God, who said, "Light shall shine out of darkness," is the One who has shone in

our hearts to give the Light of the knowledge of the
glory of God in the face of Christ.

The light God shines on us is a revelation, "the Light of the
knowledge." It is a revelation of His love. That revelation of His
love gives us life. That's what removes darkness and opens our eyes.
That's what removes death and blindness.

We all know the Father loves us because we know John 3:16, "For
God so loved the world that He gave . . ." We all know that the Son
loves us because He died for our sins. But how do we know that the
Holy Spirit loves us?

Rom 5:5 The love of God has been poured out
within our hearts through the Holy Spirit . . .

We know that the Holy Spirit loves us because He takes the Father's
love and acceptance, and Jesus' death and resurrection and makes
it personal to us, to me! He gives me a love story, a redemption that
is personal.

God removes the obstacle of blindness by giving me a revelation of
how much He loves and accepts me personally. Love and acceptance
are the answer to unfruitfulness because it is my love deficiency and
rejection that prevent my fruitfulness. I make idols of things and
people when in my ignorance I seek love and acceptance, out of my
love deficiency, in those things or people and not in God. Allow me
to illustrate how this works with a personal story.

I grew up without my mother and father. One of my aunts took
me to live with her and her husband, and a few years later I went to
live with my grandma. Needless to say, I felt abandoned all my life,
although I couldn't identify it as such at that early age. Even though
I had a great upbringing and was loved, cared and provided for, the
abandonment affected me profoundly.

One of my earliest childhood memories goes back to when I was about 5 years old. I remember the house we lived in, my aunt, her husband, their daughter and me. I remember very distinctly feeling that I didn't belong, that they weren't my real family, that I couldn't relax. Although I couldn't express it in so many words, I felt rejected, unaccepted and unacceptable. That marked me for years to come and determined so much of who I became and how I related to others. Although I was loved by many, I couldn't receive that love. I was like a plant incapable of absorbing light and water. Satan had interpreted life's hurts for me, and his interpretations, his lies, became my identity, my prison, my love deficiency. It was a love deficiency that sent me out into the world broken, seeking wholeness away from God. And even after I came to know God, I couldn't receive His love in a personal and deeply transforming way.

Unaware of this, I couldn't relax in my relationship with God. I tried to make myself more acceptable to Him by my behavior, my knowledge and my service to Him. I didn't consciously realize that I felt unaccepted by God. I was saved and understood salvation by grace alone, but I didn't understand grace to enjoy Him as my Father. A spirit of slavery dominated me, and in my bondage to sin, to the flesh and to Satan's lies, I tried to stand out more than others in order to find worth and acceptance. I tried to serve God but not out of freedom and love. I was trapped in religious performance, even though I had a relationship with God. Years and decades would pass before I finally found healing from my love deficiency and freedom from the lies about myself, God my Father, and even love itself.

A healing breakthrough came when I received a revelation of God's personal love for me and His acceptance. In a guided exercise I was led to bring to mind the earliest memory of the pain of abandonment. Then I was led to ask Jesus, "Where were you at that time, in that place, at that moment in my life?" He showed me He was there, in a corner of that terrible place were Satan's lies attacked me like a pack of wolves. But now I knew the truth, that Jesus had been there all along, and His presence transformed the place from darkness to a beautiful, peaceful blue. His presence transformed the external atmosphere and my internal experience to peace and love. I wasn't alone anymore. I wasn't unloved anymore! I asked Him, "What do you have to say to me, to that child?" God responded, "I love you! You were not an orphan. You were not abandoned. You were loved. You are my child. I am your Father!" God showed me how at that time I was loved, that He loved me. He showed me a crucial part of my experience Satan gladly misinterpreted for me as a child, that I was loved by God and by others. Understanding this love closed my wounds. It healed me. I am love deficient no more! This brought an initial freedom that has been increasing ever since and in which I continue to grow. My heart is satisfied with His love alone, and that has made me whole, no longer broken!

A personal revelation of God's love removes death and blindness, the darkness, which is the first obstacle to our fruitfulness.

CHAPTER SIX

FLOOD

Let's now talk about the second obstacle to fruitfulness, the flood. The land in Genesis 1 was covered by water. The water made the land unfruitful. God set out to remove the waters and uncover the dry ground. When He removed the waters He separated them, putting some above the space He created, and the rest of the water He confined to the oceans. In the flood of Genesis 6 to 9 the waters above came down and the fountains underground broke lose. Water covered again the whole earth, the tallest mountain peaks. The flood was an ironic reversal to unfruitfulness as consequence for man's sin. The same dynamic is present in us as land.

After His covenant promise of never again destroying the earth with a flood, God now accomplishes a reversal to unfruitfulness due to sin by turning the land into a wilderness. The wilderness then stands in place of the flood. The unfruitfulness we experience, our flood and wilderness, is due to our iniquity, the iniquity of our parents and ancestors, or both.

INIQUITY
1. Iniquities are a personal flood
Notice the connection between iniquities and a personal flood:

Ezra 9:6 And I said, "O my God, I am ashamed and embarrassed to lift up my face to You, my God, for our iniquities have risen above our heads . . .

Psa 106:43 They . . . sank down in their iniquity.

2. Iniquities are a personal wilderness

Don't miss in the following passage the connection between iniquities and a personal wilderness. Iniquities result in unfruitfulness, no rain (a drought) and no harvest (a famine). These are the characteristics of a wilderness.

> Jer 5:23-25 'But this people has a stubborn and rebellious heart; they have turned aside and departed. 'They do not say in their heart, "Let us now fear the LORD our God, who gives rain in its season, both the autumn rain and the spring rain, who keeps for us the appointed weeks of the harvest." 'Your iniquities have turned these away, and your sins have withheld good from you.

The Bible repeats time after time that God visits the iniquity of man on their children and grand children to the third and forth generations.

> Ex 20:4-5 You shall not make for yourself an idol, or any likeness of what is in heaven above or on the earth beneath or in the water under the earth. "You shall not worship them or serve them; for I, the LORD your God, am a jealous God, visiting the iniquity of the fathers on the children, on the third and the fourth generations of those who hate Me.

> Ex 34:7 He will by no means leave the guilty unpunished, visiting the iniquity of fathers on the

children and on the grandchildren to the third and
fourth generations.

This is true not only of physical children but also of spiritual
children, all those on whom our spiritual DNA is reproduced by
our influence. They suffer for our unfruitfulness, our iniquity, our
flood and wilderness.

3. Iniquity is perversion

The Hebrew word translated iniquity is "avon," and its basic meaning
is to pervert or twist something. It also includes the ideas of a
heavy burden that physically affects the person due to his or her
perversion; the heaviness of the consequences; and the heaviness of
the punishment incurred. Iniquity, the perverting and twisting that
takes place in the heart, results in a strong rejection of God and His
word. Look at a list of passages that illustrate this.

> Lev 26:40 If they confess their iniquity and the
> iniquity of their forefathers, in their unfaithfulness
> which they committed against Me, and also in their
> acting with hostility against Me.

> Lev 26:43 They, meanwhile, will be making
> amends for their iniquity, because they rejected My
> ordinances and their soul abhorred My statutes.

> Num 15:31 Because he has despised the word of
> the LORD . . . his guilt [Hebrew "avon," iniquity]
> *will be* on him

> Psa 49:5-6 the iniquity of my foes . . . who trust in
> their wealth and boast in the abundance of their
> riches . . .

> Is 1:4 Alas, sinful nation, people weighed down
> with iniquity, offspring of evildoers, sons who act

corruptly! They have abandoned the LORD, they have despised the Holy One of Israel, they have turned away from Him.

Is 57:17 Because of the iniquity of his unjust gain . . . he went on turning away, in the way of his heart.

Is 65:7 Both their own iniquities and the iniquities of their fathers together," says the LORD. Because they have . . . scorned Me . . .

Jer 11:10 "They have turned back to the iniquities of their ancestors who refused to hear My words.

Allow me to highlight these iniquities so you see up close what they are about.

Passage	Iniquities
Lev 26:40	Unfaithfulness
	Hostility against Me
Lev 26:43	Rejected My ordinances
	Abhorred My statutes
Num 15:31	Despised the word of the LORD
Psa 49:5-6	Trust in their wealth
	Boast in the abundance of their riches
Is 1:4	Abandoned the LORD
	Despised the Holy One
	Turned away from Him
Is 57:17	Turning away, in the way of his heart
Is 65:7	Scorned Me
Jer 11:10	Refused to hear My words

Iniquity is a perversion in the heart by which a person rejects God and His word, in order to follow his own way, thus bringing a burden of consequences and bondage upon himself. This perversion, burden and bondage also affect those in close association with the person, especially their children. We call this generational iniquities.

4. Iniquities have consequences
Iniquities have multiple consequences, but they all fit one description: spiritual bondage.

> Prov 5:22 His own iniquities will capture the wicked,
> and he will be held with the cords of his sin.

According to Jeremiah 33:8 the problem behind sin and transgression is iniquity:

. . . all their iniquity by which they have sinned
against Me, and . . . by which they have transgressed
against Me.

Other consequences of iniquities are:

Emotional and health issues
Psa 38:18 For I confess my iniquity; I am full of
anxiety because of my sin.

Psa 31:10 For my life is spent with sorrow and my
years with sighing; my strength has failed because
of my iniquity, and my body has wasted away.

Sword, captivity, plunder and shame
(which all have spiritual meanings as well)
Ezra 9:7 "Since the days of our fathers to this day
we have been in great guilt, and on account of our
iniquities we, our kings and our priests have been
given into the hand of the kings of the lands, to
the sword, to captivity and to plunder and to open
shame, as it is this day.

Spiritual blindness and distance from God
Psa 40:12 My iniquities have overtaken me, so that
I am not able to see . . .

Is 59:2 But your iniquities have made a separation
between you and your God, and your sins have
hidden His face from you so that He does not hear.

**Demonic activity allowed and unleashed by
God**
Jer 30:14 I have wounded you with the wound of an
enemy, with the punishment of a cruel one, because
your iniquity is great and your sins are numerous.

God's severe discipline
Psa 39:11 With reproofs You chasten a man for iniquity; you consume as a moth what is precious to him; surely every man is a mere breath.

5. Iniquities bring curses

The perversion, rejection of God and the twisted ways modeled by parents give legal right to demonic activity in their lives and in the lives of their children. The curses or consequences of these iniquities fall upon their children. The perversions become generational iniquities, and the consequences become generational curses. The word perversion sounds strong and may lead some to think, "I don't have 'perversions' in my life, and neither do my parents, grand parents or ancestors. Iniquity isn't a big deal in my family history." But look at what Isaiah says,

> Is 53:6 All of us like sheep have gone astray, each of us has turned to his own way; but the LORD has caused the iniquity of us all to fall on Him.

God visits the iniquity of the fathers up to four generations after them. This is understood popularly as God punishing sin for generations. I'd like to offer an enlightening passage we may not have considered.

> Gen 15:16 "Then in the fourth generation they will return here, for the iniquity of the Amorite is not yet complete."

In Genesis 15 God tells Abraham that his descendents would be enslaved in Egypt. God also told him that four generations after Abraham's death He would bring them back to Canaan to possess the land. God gave the Amorites, and no doubt all the inhabitants of Canaan, four generations to repent from their iniquity. And even when God came to visit the iniquity of the Canaanites, repentance was very available. Notice this familiar case.

Heb 11:31 By faith Rahab the harlot did not perish along with those who were disobedient, after she had welcomed the spies in peace.

Josh 6:23 So the young men who were spies went in and brought out Rahab and her father and her mother and her brothers and all she had; they also brought out all her relatives and placed them outside the camp of Israel.

So rich was the compassion of God on Rahab, and so profound her transformation from her iniquities, that she produced an amazing son, godly, compassionate and with great spiritual priorities. His name was Boaz.

Matt 1:5 Salmon was the father of Boaz by Rahab, Boaz was the father of Obed by Ruth, and Obed the father of Jesse.

Rahab's generational perversions and curses were radically stopped.

Visiting the iniquity of one generation on the next is letting them suffer under the burden of consequences for the perversions they have also adopted. By this visitations God mercifully attempts to deliver the next generation from that perversions and curses. He visits iniquity in order to produce repentance.

6. Iniquities are removed by the Holy Spirit
The obstacle of flood, of wilderness, is removed by freeing the person from the bondage of iniquity and its consequences.

When a person comes to know Christ they are a new creation. Just like the land of Genesis 1, they too need to be made fruitful;

the obstacles to fruitfulness need to be removed. How did God remove the obstacle of flood in Genesis 1? He did it through the Holy Spirit: "The Spirit of God was moving over the surface of the waters."[27] That was the same way He removed Noah's flood: "God caused a wind to pass over the earth, and the water subsided."[28]

I'm not saying the Holy Spirit is a "wind." However, the Hebrew word translated Spirit is the same word translated wind. This is true in Hebrew as well as in Greek. Scripture uses these meanings as play on words in order to interchange ideas. The work of the Spirit is illustrated by the wind's unseen cause and effect. God does things in the natural through the wind that are patterns of the spiritual things He does through His Spirit. Jesus Himself used this play on words when He said,

> John 3:8 "The wind blows where it wishes and you hear the sound of it, but do not know where it comes from and where it is going; so is everyone who is born of the Spirit."

The natural speaks of the spiritual. In the spiritual reality, the Holy Spirit works in such a way that He removes the personal flood of iniquities, which is over us impeding our fruitfulness. The Holy Spirit also removes our wilderness. He does it through rain.

We will explore later in greater detail the role of the wind, and the word play with the Holy Spirit, in delivering us from bondage.

The obstacle of darkness stands for death, blindness and a love deficiency. The solution is a personal revelation of God's healing love found on the cross and the empty tomb. The obstacle of flood, of wilderness, stands for the bondage of iniquity, personal and

---

27   Gen 1:2
28   Gen 8:1

generational. Its solution is the freedom found in the victory of the cross and the empty tomb. Healing and freedom are the work God desires to do in our lives, through His word and by His Spirit, to prepare us for fruitfulness.

CHAPTER SEVEN

FRUITFULNESS

After God removed darkness and flood, the dry land appeared. The land had been formed. Now it needed to be filled. God made the land fruitful so it could sustain life, so it could feed animals and people. As good as removing our death, blindness and bondage is, the process is still incomplete if we don't become fruitful people. Take a look at Jesus' teaching.

> Matt 12:43-45 Now when the unclean spirit goes out of a man, it passes through waterless places seeking rest, and does not find it. "Then it says, 'I will return to my house from which I came'; and when it comes, it finds it unoccupied, swept, and put in order. "Then it goes and takes along with it seven other spirits more wicked than itself, and they go in and live there; and the last state of that man becomes worse than the first. That is the way it will also be with this evil generation.

The house "unoccupied, swept, and put in order" still had something wrong: it was empty. The empty house was like the land after it was formed, with no obstacles to fruitfulness, yet still uninhabited, empty. What the house needed was to be occupied, filled.

Obviously, Jesus isn't just talking about real estate property; He's talking about people. He said " . . . the last state of that man . . ." The house represents the man. The man "unoccupied, swept, and put in order" means he was healed and set free from spiritual bondage. His obstacles to fruitfulness were removed. The "evil generation" that Jesus compared to the man and to the house is the same "brood of vipers" He talked about a few verses earlier. He said of them "make the tree good and its fruit good, or make the tree bad and its fruit bad."[29] "The good man brings out of his good treasure what is good; and the evil man brings out of his evil treasure what is evil."[30] Clearly, Jesus was talking about fruitfulness when referring to the house in need of being filled, occupied. In other words, He was saying, "After being healed and freed, people need to be filled with fruitfulness."

As we have shown before, the activity of seeing means that God decides what is good and provides it. Jeremiah 5:25 says that "your sins have withheld good from you." The verse before that says about God, "Who gives rain in its season, both the autumn rain and the spring rain, who keeps for us the appointed weeks of the harvest." In context, the "good" withheld was the rain and the harvest, the water that made the land fruitful. This has the same meaning in Genesis 1 where the land was very good because it was very fruitful, well watered.

That's what God wants to do in you and me. A blessed land is one that's fruitful, because God's blessing brings about fruitfulness. A blessed person is one who receives the "good" from God, water, rain, making him or her fruitful. A fruitful person is one who has been healed of his or her love deficiency and made free from bondage to iniquities, and is now receiving rain and producing a harvest of grain (the word, teachings from God), grapes (the joy of the Lord) and olives (oil, anointing, sanctification). Such land, such life, is very fruitful, very blessed, very good indeed!

---

29   Matt 12:33
30   Matt 12:35

PART II

FREEDOM

CHAPTER EIGHT

BONDAGE

The book of Exodus opens by establishing a connection with the book of Genesis. Not only does it establish continuity of narrative by resuming the story of Jacob's children living in Egypt, but it also establishes a theological continuity by advancing forward the blessing from Abraham, Isaac and Jacob.

> Ex 1:7 But the sons of Israel were fruitful and increased greatly, and multiplied, and became exceedingly mighty, so that the land was filled with them.

This verse is full of the same words God pronounced as blessing over Adam and Eve, and later repeated to Noah, Abraham, Isaac and Jacob. The one and only blessing, as we saw when Isaac blessed Jacob and not Esau, is now over all the children of Jacob, the people of Israel. And these very words of blessing are found in the lips of Pharaoh himself:

> Ex 1:9 He said to his people, "Behold, the people of the sons of Israel are more and mightier than we."

We have here two key characteristics of Hebrew narrative. First, we see the use of dialogue. And second, the use of the word "behold."

The term "behold" serves as a "signpost" from the author alerting the reader: "Attention! A key to understanding the story is coming right now!" This highlights the fact that the author has already interrupted the narrative to insert a dialogue. When the author does this he is putting key revelation of what he is trying to communicate on the lips of key characters. The dialogue and the attention getter both point to the prominence of God's blessing in the narrative. This, united to the fact that these words come out of Pharaoh's own mouth, creates a powerful and dramatic effect.

AFFLICTION

Pharaoh, unbeknown to him, is in direct opposition to God's blessing. His purpose is to disrupt God's grand agenda from taking place. This, of course, is no coincidence. Pharaoh represents Satan in this redemption pattern, because he is the boastful king opposing God. He fears Israel's fruitfulness and sets out to oppose it to the death.

> Ex 1:10 "Come, let us deal wisely with them, or else they will multiply and in the event of war, they will also join themselves to those who hate us, and fight against us and depart from the land."

The problem for Pharaoh isn't just Israel's exponential growth, or that they may join Egypt's enemies. The problem isn't even that Israel may make war on Egypt. What Pharaoh just couldn't let happen was that Israel "depart from the land." In Hebrew it literally says, "Go up from the land." That phrase does not point to just any direction, it points to the land of Canaan because in order to go from Egypt to Canaan you go up the hill country. Satan, concealed behind Pharaoh, had to prevent at all cost that Israel return to the Promised Land, to the land of blessing, the land of fruitfulness.

Pharaoh then devises a "wise," dirty plan.

Ex 1:11 So they appointed taskmasters over them to afflict them with hard labor.

In Hebrew, "taskmasters" is made-up of two words. Their respective meanings are: "princes" and "forced labor." These "princes of forced labor" forced the Israelites into slavery to Pharaoh their master. "Taskmasters" points to the forced nature of the labor, and "hard labor" at the end of the verse points to the burdensome nature of it. The intention of the hard and forced labor was to "afflict" the Jewish people. The word "afflict" means to treat someone violently in order to oppress them and humiliate them, so they would be distraught. In this case, the desired result was that, in such distraught state, Israel wouldn't procreate. Pharaoh wanted to stop this multiplication. Satan wanted to stop God's blessing.

What is this teaching us? The "taskmasters," the "princes of forced labor" are demons appointed to enslave us so we serve their master. The demons oppress people through humiliation and shame, afflicting them to suppress their fruitfulness. Their desire is to cut off God's blessing. To prevent that you and I "go up" to own our God-promised land. People live under such oppression, bondage and unfruitfulness for years!

Although Israel's affliction and bondage under Satan's taskmasters were unprovoked, many of our afflictions today are due to personal or generational iniquity.

Psa 107:17 Fools, because of their rebellious way, and because of their iniquities, were afflicted.

God, however, is compassionate to forgive our iniquity.

Psa 78:38 But He, being compassionate, forgave their iniquity and did not destroy them . . .

In the pages of the book of Acts we read of the Apostles who, though afflicted by powerful taskmasters, nonetheless thrived and multiplied! Their taskmasters where religious princes, and the taskmasters that afflict us, the demons, are religious in nature as well. Let's look into this.

RELIGIOSITY

Israel was forced to "build for Pharaoh storage cities." The names of these cities were Pithom and Raamses. The word "Pithom" means "temple of the sun." "Raamses" means "born of the sun god." The title "Pharaoh" means "big house" or "big temple." Pharaoh himself was worshiped as the son of the sun god. Satan's kingdom truly is religious in nature. It's all about worship: worshipping him. And he wants to enslave people so they serve him, building his house, his temple, thus preventing their fruitfulness.

The structures built by the Jewish slaves where places to store grain. Pharaoh didn't want Israel to possess their own land and harvest their own grain. The grain stored no doubt was wheat and barley, both used to make bread.

The believer in bondage doesn't own him or herself, doesn't possess his land. Therefore, he has no grain, no bread of his own. He doesn't have the Word. Sure, he is religious, that's what Satan wants us to be, to store "his bread." Many believers have doctrine and theology, but they don't have "a word" from God that is fresh and alive. They may have biblical principles, but not a direct word right for the moment. They don't have a harvest of truth taught to them by the Holy Spirit. This isn't meant to point a finger at anyone. In fact, finger pointing is one of Satan's preferred religious tools.

The "taskmasters," the "princes of forced labor" in our lives, the demons assigned to beat us and shame us, do so primarily by finger pointing, by accusations. After all, Satan is the accuser of the brethren. The demons afflict, torment, shame and humiliate us by accusing us. Their lies frequently take the form of accusations. These accusations are very religious in nature, and that's why they are so deceptive, powerful and effective. We think it's just our own voice, or even worse, we think is God or the Holy Spirit speaking to us. These accusations take the form of exhortations to behave better, but they don't originate in God's redemptive compassion, empowering grace and dignifying love. Rather, they originate in a false conditional acceptance by God. These accusations take the form of self-insults and put-downs, telling yourself how stupid you are. Tons of preaching and teaching based on shame are nothing but the words of a person who is oppressed and shamed, "ministering" shame and oppression. The "logic" of it all is twisted, and yet because it appeals to our human religious nature, we buy into it as truth. The "taskmasters" would have us do a lot of busy work "for God," "serving Him," "walking with Him," but religiosity is a counterfeit of real fruitfulness, actually a bondage to Satan and to the flesh. Not pleasing to God.

Those "taskmasters" also love to accuse and misrepresent God to you. "God is angry at you. What happened to you is judgment for what you did, or didn't do. God is like a bad human father. Can't be trusted. Doesn't really care. He always blesses and helps others, not you. He's unfair." All of this is to make you "serve" God as a slave in bondage, out of fear of punishment and not in freedom, not as a son. Satan's aim is that you and I become religious hypocrites, not people who love others as God loves us. The goal is that you and I never become victorious but always live under sin's thumb. Never becoming fruitful, experiencing the blessing of God.

How do we stop the voices? How do we stop the accusing and insulting voices? How do we stop this affliction? Stay tuned. That's what Exodus is all about. It ties up with Genesis and what we've said so far.

Meanwhile Pharaoh, even with such oppression, couldn't stop God's blessing.

Ex 1:12 But the more they afflicted them, the more they multiplied and the more they spread out, so that they were in dread of the sons of Israel.

Pharaoh was just warming up, though.

Ex 1:13-14 The Egyptians compelled the sons of Israel to labor rigorously; and they made their lives bitter with hard labor in mortar and bricks and at all kinds of labor in the field, all their labors which they rigorously imposed on them.

In Hebrew, verse 13 literally says, "Egypt, ruthlessly (harshly, brutally), made Israel serve as slaves." The lives of the Israelites were bitter. Not in the sense that they were full of unforgiveness, but in the sense of great emotional distress. The word "hard" in "hard labor" (v. 14) is one of the Hebrew words used for Pharaoh's "hardened" heart. Such hard heart was the source of his ruthless hard labor. Israel was also forced to work in the fields. That speaks of agriculture: grain and bread, representing teaching. These are religious teachings, commandments of men and exhortations that bring about bondage, promoted by the believer who is oppressed and under spiritual bondage.

LEADERSHIP

Pharaoh kept thinking, and soon Satan whispered a plan that just couldn't fail. In an attempt to attack the men of Israel, all that represents multiplication, initiative and leadership, Pharaoh tries to intimidate those who assist women in giving birth.

Ex 1:15-16 Then the king of Egypt spoke to the Hebrew midwives, one of whom was named Shiphrah and the other was named Puah; and he said, "When you are helping the Hebrew women to give birth and **see** them upon the birthstool, if it is a son, then you shall **put him to death**; but if it is a daughter, then **she shall live**."[31]

Pharaoh said to them, "See . . . kill . . . let live!" Precisely what Satan wants us to do, that we take matters into our own hands, taking from God the activity of "seeing." The intention is that we bring death to God's blessing and fruitfulness in us and in others. But the midwives didn't obey the commandments of men. They saw the spiritual nature of it, that it went against God. The commandments of men are religious in nature and they proceed from the "taskmasters," demonic forces, who try to intimidate us and take away our initiative, our leadership, and our fruitfulness. The midwives would not become agents and accomplices against God's blessing of multiplication.

> Ex 1:20 So God was good to the midwives, and the people multiplied, and became very mighty.

It is interesting that God wanted us to know the names of the midwives. Why? What for? I'm sure one of the reasons was to give us a teaching, of course! The name "Shiphra" means "Beautiful." "The word seems to imply the sense that this is the way something should be when it is right or at its best."[32] This woman was "Beautiful" because all was right in her life, because she was at her best, that is, being what God created her to be, a top midwife who hears God. And the other woman's name, Puah, means "Glitter." The root of this word implies something shattered, with the particles now shining, glittering. In that we can see a painful experience, we can see someone now healed and overcoming, and as a midwife we can see in her the multiplication and joy brought to others.

As midwives, both of them assisted those who gave birth, who gave life. Satan wanted to strike the people of God at that high and

---

[31] Emphasis added.
[32] *NIDOTTE*, s.v. "shafar shefer shifrah," 4:228.

critical level. So it is in the kingdom. Those leaders of leaders, the ones God has appointed to assist those who give birth and give life, are intimidated by Satan to "see," independently of God. They are intimidated to make decisions that could bring death to blessing and fruitfulness in themselves and others. This doesn't just apply to the pastor of a mega church. This also applies to a mom and a dad who have children in their hands, whose fruitfulness, or absence of it, will be determined by what their parents feed them. And this applies to leaders at every stage and in every field, to anyone who has influence over others.

CHAPTER NINE

PROVIDENCE

God's providence, in great part, has to do with God using Satan to defeat Satan. God uses Satan's attacks to defeat Satan. In retrospect, these instances are divine, ironic reversals. Frustrated that his "wise" plans were not working out, Pharaoh, and Satan pulling the strings behind him, barks out this categorical order.

> Ex 1:22 Every son who is born you are to cast into the Nile . . .

What's ironic about this, and providential, is that Pharaoh's own daughter not only rescues a little Jewish boy from death in blatant disregard for his edict, but the boy is actually "drawn out of the waters"! She named him Moses (Hebrew Moshe), and said, "Because I drew (masha) him out of the water."[33] The waters, the very instrument of death ordered by Satan, became a point of resurrection (as it were) for the baby boy, the future leader of the people of God! Ironic! Providential!

The psalmist says,

> Psa 18:16 He sent from on high, He took me; He drew (masha) me out of many waters.

---

[33]   Ex 2:10

God rescued Noah and his family out of the waters of judgment, and He will rescue Israel parting the sea, and judge Egypt in the waters. And God will use a man "drawn" out of the waters to accomplish this.

Let's now fast-forward to Moses at the burning bush.

> Ex 3:1-4 Now Moses was pasturing the flock of Jethro his father-in-law, the priest of Midian; and he led the flock to the west side of the wilderness and came to Horeb, the mountain of God. The angel of the LORD appeared to him in a blazing fire from the midst of a bush; and he looked, and behold, the bush was burning with fire, yet the bush was not consumed. So Moses said, "I must turn aside now and see this marvelous sight, why the bush is not burned up." When the LORD saw that he turned aside to look, God called to him from the midst of the bush and said, "Moses, Moses!" And he said, "Here I am."

Israel was the bush that wouldn't burn, even though it was experiencing a fiery demonic attack. God was both in the flame of fire and in the middle of the bush. When a servant of God sees people in affliction, bitter suffering and under "taskmasters," he or she must also be able to see that God is in their midst and even in their fire of demonic bondage. When a servant of God has such compassion, God can send him or her to bring deliverance to people!

THE STAFF

Here's a summary of Moses' exchange with God while being commissioned.

Moses' excuses and God's answers:
1. **Moses:** Who am I?
   God: I will deliver you
2. **Moses:** What shall I tell them your name is?
   God:
   a. I am who I am (self existing), the Sacred Name,[34] God of the patriarchs
   b. Tell Israel: I care about you, I'll bring you up from Egypt
   c. They'll hear you and come with you to Pharaoh
   d. I will strike Egypt to let you go
   e. You won't leave empty-handed
3. **Moses:** What if they don't listen but say, "God didn't appear to you"?
   God:
   a. The staff and the serpent
   b. The "leprous" (*tsaraat*[35]) hand
   c. Water into blood
4. **Moses:** I won't know what to say!
   God: I've opened your mouth. I'll teach you what to say.
5. **Moses:** I really don't want to go!
   God: I'll send your brother to go with you.

What we know today as leprosy isn't the same as biblical "leprosy." What we see in the Bible is a series of skin diseases. I use here the Hebrew term *tsaraat* as is used in the Jewish world. In the book of Leviticus we learn that *tsaraat* is the second highest form of impurity, the first being death. The reason for this is that these skin diseases make the person have the appearance of a corpse.

---

[34] Jewish people don't pronounce this name. They say "Adonai," which means "Lord" in substitution. When English Bibles use the all capitals LORD, the Hebrew word is the Sacred Name of God. They also call God "Hashem" which is Hebrew for "The Name." The New Testament writers followed this tradition and even Jesus' phrase "the kingdom of heaven" was a way to avoid pronouncing the Sacred Name. We follow the same in this book.

[35] See explanation in the paragraph below the summary.

The *tsaraat* in Moses' hand ties in with the water turned into blood. Leviticus teaches that the life is in the blood. However, when Moses strikes the Nile the waters will turn into blood like a man slain and bleeding to death. We see the theme of death in those two signs, blood and *tsaraat*. God is sovereign over life and death and He gave Moses that authority.

How then does the staff that turns into serpent fit in with blood and *tsaraat*? The serpent stands for Satan, leader of the forces of death.

Notice that Moses executes God's judgments through the staff. As we've said, God uses Satan to defeat Satan. The plagues over Egypt, introduced in most instances by Moses' staff, represent demonic activity, used by God, to bring judgment over Pharaoh, Satan's own representative. God uses demonic forces to bring judgment over Satan's kingdom. This is divine, ironic reversal.[36] Take, for instance, the plague of locusts. We know from other parts of Scriptures that the locusts represent demons, and that they come by God's judgment. We have the same representation in Exodus. Moses was sent to Pharaoh,[37] who in turn represents Satan. Moses was sent with the power of demonic judgment and death, to bring judgment and death to Satan and his taskmasters. He had in his hand the judgment of God to defeat Satan and his taskmasters, thus freeing Israel from bondage.

The person who ministers freedom from afflictions to others must contend with the taskmasters, applying God's judgments of them, to set the afflicted free from bondage. The bondage comes by iniquity, a willful rejection and rebellion against God (even if it is passive, came as a child or is generational), and chasing after idols. Most

---

[36] This is just like what God would do many times to enemy armies attacking Israel, turning them against each other. Jesus said in Mark 3:25-26, "If a house is divided against itself, that house will not be able to stand. "If Satan has risen up against himself and is divided, he cannot stand, but he is finished!" God uses this principle to defeat Satan.

[37] Exodus 3:10: "Therefore, come now, and I will send you to Pharaoh."

of these idols originate in a love deficiency, and the person needs healing. Freedom comes easily once the person is healed. Freedom is unlocked by taking away Satan's legal rights over the person. This is done through repentance ("every man will turn from his evil way; then I will forgive their iniquity.").[38] God forgives iniquity. He releases the person from iniquity's burden[39] by lifting and carrying[40] Himself[41] the burden.

Freedom comes through redemption. It is through redemption that Satan's right was taken away. We will explain in the following chapters how God redeems people and sets them free.

ILLUSTRATION

The principle of God using Satan to defeat Satan is dramatically illustrated in David's life. Look carefully at the following parallel passages:

> 2 Sam 24:1-2 Now again **the anger of the LORD** burned against Israel, and it **incited** David against them to say, "Go, number Israel and Judah." The king said to Joab the commander of the army who was with him, "Go about now through all the tribes of Israel, from Dan to Beersheba, and register the people, that I may know the number of the people."[42]

> 1 Chr 21:1-2 **Then Satan** stood up against Israel and **moved** David to number Israel. So David said to

---

[38] Jer 36:3

[39] Ex 34:9 "and pardon our iniquity." The Hebrew word translated "pardon" means "release."

[40] Hosea 14:2 "Take words with you and return to the LORD. Say to Him, "Take away all iniquity." The phrase "take away" means in Hebrew "to lift, to carry," and sometimes is translated "forgive."

[41] Is 53:11 "As He will bear their iniquities." This talks of Jesus at the cross.

[42] Emphasis added.

Joab and to the princes of the people, "Go, number Israel from Beersheba even to Dan, and bring me *word* that I may know their number."[43]

The words "incited," and "moved" are translations of the same Hebrew word. The manifestation of God's anger in judging oppressors and disciplining His children comes by God unleashing demonic activity on them. So much so that Satan is equaled to God's anger. Even when God's discipline is not due to sin He uses satanic attacks. Job and Paul are the best human examples of that, and Jesus is the ultimate example.

> Ps 78:49-50 He sent upon them His burning anger, fury and indignation and trouble, a band of destroying angels. He leveled a path for His anger; He did not spare their soul from death, but gave over their life to the plague,

God's burning anger is the same as a band of destroying demons. Note in the next passage how God uses demons:

> 1 Kings 22:19-23 Micaiah said, "Therefore, hear the word of the LORD. I saw the LORD sitting on His throne, and all the host of heaven standing by Him on His right and on His left. "The LORD said, 'Who will entice Ahab to go up and fall at Ramoth-gilead?' And one said this while another said that. "Then a spirit came forward and stood before the LORD and said, 'I will entice him.' "The LORD said to him, 'How?' And he said, 'I will go out and be a deceiving spirit in the mouth of all his prophets.' Then He said, 'You are to entice *him* and also prevail. Go and do so.' "Now therefore, behold, the LORD has put a deceiving spirit in the

---

[43] Emphasis added.

mouth of all these your prophets; and the LORD
has proclaimed disaster against you."

God applied this same principle in Solomon's life.

> 1 Kings 11:9, 14, 23 Now the LORD was angry with
> Solomon because his heart was turned away from
> the LORD, the God of Israel . . . Then the LORD
> raised up an **adversary** to Solomon, Hadad the
> Edomite . . . God also raised up *another* **adversary**
> to him, Rezon the son of Eliada.[44]

In order to bring Solomon to repentance God raised up "adversaries"
to him. The Hebrew word translated "adversary" twice in this
passage is "satan." Our English word "Satan" comes straight from
the Hebrew word "satan," which as we know means "adversary." But
as Ephesians 6 teaches us, even when the adversaries are human, the
real battle is spiritual. All the human opposition Jesus faced in His
life was really a spiritual battle, and He fought it as such.

Does God raise adversaries against us? All the time! For what
purpose? In order to produce fruitfulness in us!

God grants Satan the right to attack us. This right may or may not
be based on our iniquities and sins. God's purpose is to use Satan to
defeat Satan in our lives, to bring judgment to Satan in our lives so
we can have freedom and be fruitful. Job was twice as fruitful after
his ordeal. Have you ever come across people against whom God has
raised adversaries? All the time! We must be very discerning. Such
people can be our own children, spouse, relatives, friends, students,
coworkers, etc. We must hear God and proceed just as He instructs
us because He wants to use that very attack, somehow, to bring
unprecedented victory. Knowing this we can be a definitive factor in
completing God's judgment over Satan in the lives of people.

---

[44]   Emphasis added.

CHAPTER TEN

PAYMENT

The book of Exodus relates the story of God's redemption of the people of Israel from Pharaoh in Egypt. The book is a pattern of how God redeems people from bondage and brings them to fruitfulness.

The concept of redemption has several components: payment, bondage and freedom. In general, we can say that redemption is delivering from bondage by paying the price of freedom. Deliverance is at the heart of redemption. Let's look at the Old Testament's teaching about redemption and see how vital it is for our fruitfulness. We will then explore those principles in the exodus from Egypt.

Just as Genesis 1 is a pattern of how God makes us fruitful as land, so the exodus is a pattern of how God redeems people. That pattern is seen in the New Testament's teaching about redemption, and it is seen even within the Old Testament itself. The Babylonian exile of the Jewish people is compared time after time with the exodus from Egypt.

> Is 52:4-5 For thus says the Lord GOD, "My people went down at the first into Egypt to reside there; then the Assyrian oppressed them without cause. "Now therefore, what do I have here," declares the

LORD, "seeing that My people have been taken away without cause?"

Judah, the southern kingdom, was "taken away without a cause" to captivity in Babylon. The same is true of Israel, the northern kingdom, taken by the Assyrians. And all Israel was oppressed in Egypt, even though they went to Egypt as a free people. One can argue that Judah and Israel went to captivity because of their sin, and that it wasn't "without a cause." However, that apparent contradiction is solved when we learn that this phrase can also be translated as "without compensation." Babylon took all the treasures of the land and the temple, and took captive the people of Israel. They didn't have to pay anyone for it. They just took all they wanted, plundering the people of God, all for free, without compensating anyone for it all. Assyria and Egypt did the same. That gives God the right to say:

> Is 52:3 "You were sold for nothing and you will be redeemed without money."

The phrase "for nothing" is the same in Hebrew as "without a cause, without compensation." Scripture teaches this elsewhere:

> Jer 15:13-14 "Your wealth and your treasures I will give for booty without cost [price], even for all your sins and within all your borders. "Then I will cause your enemies to bring it into a land you do not know [captive to Babylon].

> Psa 44:12 You sell Your people cheaply, and have not profited by their sale.

> Is 45:13 He [king Cyrus] will build My city and will let My exiles go free, without any payment or reward . . ."

Cyrus conquered Babylon and established the Medo-Persian Empire, and he, prompted by God, decreed that Israel could return to their land from the Babylonian captivity. Cyrus was God's instrument to judge Babylon and to let Israel go free from their oppression.

The question then is, what did God pay to redeem Israel from Babylon? And even further, to whom did He make that payment? Read carefully now:

> Is 59:17-18 He (God) put on garments of vengeance for clothing and wrapped Himself with zeal as a mantle. According to their deeds, so He will repay, **wrath** to His adversaries, recompense to His enemies; to the coastlands He will make recompense.[45]

> Jer 50:34 "Their Redeemer is strong, the LORD of hosts is His name; He will vigorously plead their case so that He may bring rest to the earth, but **turmoil** to the inhabitants of Babylon.[46]

> Is 63:4 For the day of **vengeance** was in My heart, and My year of redemption has come.[47]

The payment for redemption is vengeance, wrath, turmoil; in one word, judgment. God makes the payment of redemption to His enemies, the ones oppressing His people. Do you see these same principles in the exodus from Egypt? They are very clear, and we will see them in detail.

---

[45] Emphasis added.
[46] Emphasis added.
[47] Emphasis added.

CHAPTER ELEVEN

POWER

Redemption has a price, and that price is judgment. The price is paid to God's enemies and is brought about by God's power. God redeems people through His great power. He brings His redeeming judgment by His "mighty hand," and by His "outstretched arm." These are His signs and wonders.

> Ex 6:6 "Say, therefore, to the sons of Israel . . . 'I will also redeem you with an outstretched arm and with great judgments.

> Deut 4:34 "Or has a god tried to go to take for himself a nation from within another nation by trials, by signs and wonders and by war and by a mighty hand and by an outstretched arm and by great terrors, as the LORD your God did for you in Egypt before your eyes?

> Jer 32:21 'You brought Your people Israel out of the land of Egypt with signs and with wonders, and with a strong hand and with an outstretched arm and with great terror.

The references are to the ten plagues God brought upon Egypt, the signs and wonders He told Moses to perform. The staff God gave Moses represents God's outstretched arm with which He struck Egypt. God does this to deliver His people from those who oppress them. God uses Satan to defeat Satan, by using His staff, His outstretched arm.

> Deut 7:19 The great trials which your eyes saw and the signs and the wonders and the mighty hand and the outstretched arm by which the LORD your God brought you out. **So shall the LORD your God do to all the peoples of whom you are afraid.**[48]

Just as God had delivered Israel from Egypt, He will also deliver them from the Canaanite nations. The exodus was a pattern of how God redeems people all the time. This, of course, is how God deals with all His enemies, with Satan and his taskmasters. The nations, as Israel's enemies, represent and are empowered by the forces of evil.

> Ex 15:14-16 "The peoples have heard, they tremble; anguish has gripped the inhabitants of Philistia. "Then the chiefs of Edom were dismayed; the leaders of Moab, trembling grips them; all the inhabitants of Canaan have melted away. "Terror and dread fall upon them; by the greatness of Your arm they are motionless as stone; until Your people pass over, O LORD, until the people pass over whom You have purchased.

These nations act before the arm of the Lord, His signs and wonders of judgment, just as the demons acted when Jesus came freeing people with signs and wonders. The demons knew their coming judgment and begged Jesus not to execute it on them just yet. What Jesus did was to bring now an anticipation of that future victory,

---

[48] Emphasis added.

of that future final judgment and deliverance. That certain future victory is the power of the kingdom, the power of signs and wonders. Through a foretaste of that victory, God brings defeat to Satan and brings people into freedom from bondage.

Signs and wonders occur when we apply the judgment God has already executed on His enemies at the cross, in order to minister healing and freedom to people. Signs and wonders are God's redeeming judgment. They are God's staff in our hand to execute judgment over spiritual oppressors and bring healing and freedom.

When Pharaoh's magicians couldn't replicate Moses' miracles, performed through the staff, they said, "This is the finger of God."[49] "The finger of God" performed those miracles, His "strong hand," His "outstretched arm." Jesus defines for us what the "finger of God" is, or rather, Who the "finger of God" is.

> Luke 11:20 "But if I cast out demons by the finger of God, then the kingdom of God has come upon you.

> Matt. 12:28 "But if I cast out demons by the Spirit of God, then the kingdom of God has come upon you.

The Holy Spirit is the Finger of God! He delivers people from the hand (the power) of Pharaoh and his gods, the power of Satan and his demons.

> Deut 7:8 The LORD brought you out by a mighty hand and redeemed you from the house of slavery, from the hand of Pharaoh king of Egypt.

---

[49] Ex 8:19

Psa 106:10 So He saved them from the hand of the one who hated them, and redeemed them from the hand of the enemy.

2 Sam 7:23 Your people whom You have redeemed for Yourself from Egypt, from nations and their gods?

Mic 4:10 . . . you will go out of the city, dwell in the field, and go to Babylon. There you will be rescued; there the LORD will redeem you from the hand of your enemies.

The word translated "field" in Micah is used in Genesis 2 and 3 to describe life outside of the garden of Eden, outside the presence of God. Israel in captivity was "out of the city," out of the protective walls established by God, dwelling in the field, outside of God's presence. They were indeed in Babylon, in captivity. A person in such condition is in the hands of his or her enemy, in his power, in his grip. But the Lord rescues and redeems people out of such pit.

Psa 103:4 Who redeems your life from the pit, who crowns you with lovingkindness and compassion;

God redeems people from the burden and distress of their iniquity, from their personal flood, by the Finger of God, the Holy Spirit.

Psa 130:8 And He will redeem Israel from all his iniquities.

Ex 6:7 you shall know that I am the LORD your God, who brought you out from under the burdens [Hebrew "avon"] of the Egyptians.

Psa 69:16-19 Answer me, O LORD, for Your lovingkindness is good; according to the greatness of Your compassion, turn to me, and do not hide

Your face from Your servant, for I am in distress; answer me quickly. Oh draw near to my soul and redeem it; ransom me because of my enemies! You know my reproach and my shame and my dishonor; all my adversaries are before You.

God redeems and delivers people from the reproach, that is, the accusations of the taskmasters who come to make people feel shame and dishonor.

The person who has been set free from bondage, from oppression, is compassionate and non-judgmental toward those who are enslaved to sin and Satan.

Deut 24:17-18 "You shall not pervert the justice due an alien or an orphan, nor take a widow's garment in pledge. But you shall remember that you were a slave in Egypt, and that the LORD your God redeemed you from there; therefore I am commanding you to do this thing.

The alien, the orphan and the widow all had one thing in common: they owned no land in Israel and had no social protection. Spiritually speaking, many people do not possess their own "land," their hearts and lives are captive, under the power of the enemy, under shame and dishonor through the accusations of the taskmasters. Justice in the Torah means to make compassionate decisions, decisions that bring restitution to one under oppression. That's the heart of God, and that's what Jesus taught.

In summary, through redemption God delivers people in bondage by paying the price for their freedom. That price is judgment to the oppressors. God repays His enemies by His signs and wonders, His redeeming judgment. With this foundation we are now prepared to study the exodus itself and see more in detail God's pattern for redeeming oppressed people.

CHAPTER TWELVE

COMPASSION

DELIVERING PEOPLE FROM OPPRESSION

God is a defender of the oppressed and a deliverer of those in bondage. Even when people get themselves into a pit all on their own, God works in such a way as to prompt them to cry out to Him for help. God delights in saving people. Why? Because He is compassionate. For God compassion isn't just feeling sorry for a person, His compassion moves Him to action as well. He loves to rescue people that have fallen into a pit. God is the "Good Samaritan," if you will, who goes out of His way to help fools like us whose walk causes us to fall prey to the thieve of our souls. He carries us, cleanses and heals our wounds. God is the Father of the Prodigal, not hardened like the older brother because of our sin against Him. He runs toward us just as soon as He sees us on the road of repentance. He doesn't reproach us for our past, our foolishness and rejection of Him. He honors us with a ring, clothes our nakedness, our shame, throws a party and celebrates that we've come back to life! God also is our Judge when we, like the woman caught in the act, are guilty of all kinds of adulteries and unfaithfulness. He rebukes our oppressors and rescues us right from the grip of their clutches. He silences the accusing voices. He doesn't point the finger and warn, "I saved you this time, but don't do it again. If you do, you're on your own!" Rather, He makes us His sons and daughters, royal heirs, so we won't fall into bondage again.

The book of Exodus reveals both, God's feelings of compassion toward His oppressed people, as well as His actions to remedy their situation. Exodus describes again and again, in multiple terms, God's feelings of compassion for Israel in their distress, and how proactive He was about it. A person under oppression needs repeated compassionate reassurance and concrete actions.

> Ex 2:23-25 And the sons of Israel sighed because of the bondage, and they cried out; and their cry for help because of *their* bondage rose up to God. So God heard their groaning; and God remembered His covenant with Abraham, Isaac, and Jacob. God saw the sons of Israel, and God took notice *of them.*

God sees and hears their affliction, He is aware of their sufferings.

> Ex 3:7 The LORD said, "I have surely seen the affliction of My people who are in Egypt, and have given heed to their cry because of their taskmasters, for I am aware of their sufferings.

Remember what seeing means? It means to evaluate and decide what's beneficial for fruitfulness, and then providing that which is beneficial. A cry for help is a humble request for deliverance, for relief, and hearing is acting on that request. God knows our suffering, He is aware of it. In Jesus, God experienced demonic oppression first hand more than anyone ever has or ever will.

One of God's purposes in this text is to instill in His servant Moses the same compassion He had.

> Ex 3:9-10 "Now, behold, the cry of the sons of Israel has come to Me; furthermore, I have seen the oppression with which the Egyptians are oppressing them. "Therefore, come now, and I will send you to

Pharaoh, so that you may bring My people, the sons of Israel, out of Egypt."

The person who leads others, who evangelizes, disciples, mentors, teaches, encourages and counsels others, even if just as a friend, a parent, a school teacher, or a peer, needs to have this kind of compassion. Just like God sees and hears, we need to have our eyes and ears opened by Him and to Him in order to see and hear another person's affliction and suffering. Only then can we understand and discern how the taskmasters are causing affliction and suffering, and how God wants to set them free.

God's compassion is very personal:

Ex 3:16 I am indeed concerned about you . . .

God's compassion is very objective:

Ex 3:16 I am indeed concerned about . . . what has been done to you . . .

When God sent His human agents, Moses and Aaron, to minister freedom from bondage and affliction to Israel, He sent them with three things: words, miracles and compassion.

Ex 4:29-31 Then Moses and Aaron went and assembled all the elders of the sons of Israel; and Aaron spoke all the **words** which the LORD had spoken to Moses. He then performed the **signs** in the sight of the people. So the people believed; and when they heard that the LORD was **concerned** about the sons of Israel and that He had seen their affliction, then they bowed low and worshiped.

Notice the powerful results of that ministry strategy: they believed the word because of the confirming signs, and they worshipped

God because He showed them compassion. These three components bring balance to ministry. Teaching alone, or prophecy alone is not enough. Miracles and signs alone, or even together with prophecy, are not enough. The person ministering will see this kind of result only when they share and show the same deep compassion of God for the person and their affliction. Then they will be prepared to deliver a word from God confirmed by His signs and miracles, His redeeming judgment. By sharing God's heart of compassion He enables a person to hear what He wants to say to those oppressed by the taskmasters.

Finally, God's compassion isn't just feelings of empathy that may be expressed in kind words. James and John denounced this:

> James 2:15-16 If a brother or sister is without clothing and in need of daily food, and one of you says to them, "Go in peace, be warmed and be filled," and yet you do not give them what is necessary for *their* body, what use is that?

> 1 John 3:16-18 We know love by this, that He laid down His life for us; and we ought to lay down our lives for the brethren. But whoever has the world's goods, and sees his brother in need and closes his heart against him, how does the love of God abide in him? Little children, let us not love with word or with tongue, but in deed and truth.

God's compassion always leads to the best actions to bring about freedom from affliction. Take a close look at Exodus 6. These verses are used in the Passover service as the basis for the Four Cups traditionally drank during the meal. This is known as the "I wills" of God. Notice the seven promises, the seven "I wills":

> Ex 6:6-8 "Say, therefore, to the sons of Israel, 'I am the LORD, and **I will bring you out** from under

the burdens of the Egyptians, and **I will deliver you** from their bondage. **I will also redeem you** with an outstretched arm and with great judgments. 'Then **I will take you for My people**, and **I will be your God**; and you shall know that I am the LORD your God, who brought you out from under the burdens of the Egyptians. '**I will bring you to the land** which I swore to give to Abraham, Isaac, and Jacob, **and I will give it to you** *for* a possession; I am the LORD.'"[50]

These seven phrases are seven promises, seven actions expressed in seven verbs. Just as seven is the number of fullness, so God will take full action on behalf of His people. These are the same actions He takes on our behalf too! God deals with the taskmasters' burdens of iniquity. He delivers us from bondage to them. He pays the price of redemption, judgment to our oppressors. He becomes a Father to us taking away the spirit of slavery and giving us the Spirit of adoption, so that we are His people and He our God. He brings us to fruitfulness as land and gradually conquers that land for our possession. What God desires and promises to do is to give us a rags to riches kind of spiritual story!

God's compassion is the basis for the exodus, and it is the basis for our deliverance from bondage to Satan's taskmasters.

---

50   Emphasis added.

CHAPTER THIRTEEN

OPPRESSION

A HARDENED HEART: DETERMINED TO OPPRESS

A major feature in the exodus story is, of course, Pharaoh's hardened heart. As Scripture teaches, "our struggle is not against flesh and blood, but against the rulers, against the powers, against the world forces of this darkness, against the spiritual *forces* of wickedness in the heavenly *places*."[51] Behind Pharaoh's hard heart was Satan's determination to oppress Israel. What can all this teach us about Satan and his taskmasters' oppression? I've derived 12 principles from Pharaoh's hardened heart that apply to spiritual oppression.

1. Behind every human oppressor there is a spiritual oppressor

All oppression ultimately comes from a spiritual source, and some oppression comes through another human being. Satan can oppress a person with or without people involved. He can do it directly as a spiritual attack, or he can use a human oppressor for his spiritual attacks. That's one thing Ephesians 6:12 teaches us. Demons afflict people, put them in chains, take them captive, place them under heavy burdens and in prison. They can do that through people. People can and do oppress one another, and when they do that

---

[51]   Eph 6:12

Satan and his taskmasters are always behind it all. Paul gives us that piece of information so we know the battle is spiritual. Pharaoh's oppression of God's people is a premier illustration of this. Let's learn through this how to identify when a person is oppressed, how a person brings oppression to another and how God deals with the oppression and the oppressor.

2. A hard heart oppresses by denying freedom to others
Way before Moses went to speak to Pharaoh, the Lord told him Pharaoh would not let Israel go.

> Ex 3:19 "But I know that the king of Egypt will not permit you to go . . .

The word "permit" translates the Hebrew "natan," which means "to give." The verb "to go" is the Hebrew "halach," which means "to walk," and it's the regular word used for the spiritual walk of the believer. Pharaoh was not giving Israel the liberty to walk away free. Spiritually, Satan and his taskmasters were not giving Israel their spiritual walk. Satan had paralyzed Israel. By holding a believer captive and enslaved, Satan takes hostage their spiritual walk. This word for walk is the same one used of Enoch: he "walked with God."[52] It's also used of Noah[53] and Abraham: "Walk before Me, and be blameless."[54] Our walk, our godly lifestyle in the freedom and fruitfulness of the Spirit, is impossible to live when we're under bondage to sin and Satan. Satan uses religion and religious oppressors to hold people hostage and he doesn't give them back their true spiritual walk so they don't truly serve God.

> Ex 4:23 "So I said to you, 'Let My son go that he may serve Me'; but you have refused to let him go.

---

[52] Gen 5:22
[53] Gen 6:9
[54] Gen 17:1

"Refuse" has three possible scenarios according to its Hebrew definition. It can be use to express the rejection of an offer, to deny a request or to refuse to obey an order.[55] This last case is what we see in Pharaoh. God issued him an order, "Let My son go . . ." This is an imperative in Hebrew, a command. Pharaoh later said, "Who is the LORD that I should obey His voice to let Israel go?"[56] Pharaoh refused to free Israel.

That very command reveals the nature of Pharaoh's refusal. When God said to Pharaoh, "Let My son go that he may serve Me," the word "go" is different than in Ex 3:19, and is commonly translated "send." When someone is free you simply send them, but when you are restricting their freedom the order is to "let them go!" "Stop denying them their walk!" That's what an oppressor does. A parent, a pastor, a teacher, a spouse, a babysitter etc., can act in this way, denying someone to walk in freedom.

Pharaoh did this because his heart was hard. Exodus 7:14 says his heart was "stubborn."

> Then the LORD said to Moses, "Pharaoh's heart is stubborn; he refuses to let the people go."

The Hebrew word "kaved," translated here as "stubborn," is the same word translated many times in Scripture as "glory, honor." As an action it means to glorify, to give honor. The root word means "heavy, weighty." God's glory speaks of how heavy is the immensity of who He is. A man's honor speaks of his importance. But when used of body parts, this word means "unresponsive."[57] Pharaoh's heart was so heavy with self-importance that it was "unresponsive." It was emotionally unmovable. It didn't respond to a command from God, it didn't respond to the emotional suffering of millions

---

55 *NIDOTTE*, s.v. "Ma'an," 3:824.
56 Ex 5:2
57 NIDOTTE, s.v. "Kabed" 3:569.

of people turned slaves, it was so shut down emotionally that he ordered the killing of new born babies. After the plague of locust Pharaoh's own servants appealed to him saying, "Let the men go, that they may serve the LORD their God. Do you not realize that Egypt is destroyed?"[58] But that was to no avail. Pharaoh's heart was so hardened and emotionally unresponsive that not even the destruction of his own country moved him. Hardened people are that way. You can appeal to them but they don't show compassion for others. So are Satan and his cruel demons.

Oppressors don't let their emotions get in the way of their determination. Pharaoh "was not willing to let them go."[59] The word "willing" means to agree or consent by way of yielding. This is a will, a determination to deny freedom to others.

Even after being forced by God's plagues to let Israel go, Pharaoh couldn't hold back being who he really was in his heart:

> Ex 14:5 When the king of Egypt was told that the people had fled, Pharaoh and his servants had a change of heart toward the people . . .

The heart was never moved, softened, it was just forced, and as soon as he realized what he'd done, Pharaoh "changed" his heart back to his emotionally unmovable self. The word "change" is in a reflexive conjugation. Reflexive is when I act upon myself, like when "I shave myself." Pharaoh changed his own heart, how he felt about the people being free.

When a person is so locked down emotionally, so determined to oppress others, even if blinded to what they are doing, there's only one way to deal with that. Let's look at what that way is in our next principle.

---

[58] Ex 10:7
[59] Ex 10:27

3. Force must be used against oppressors

From the beginning, God told Moses that Pharaoh would let the people go only by force.

> Ex 3:19-20 "But I know that the king of Egypt will not permit you to go, except under compulsion. "So I will stretch out My hand and strike Egypt with all My miracles which I shall do in the midst of it; and after that he will let you go.

The phrase translated "under compulsion" literally means in Hebrew "by a strong hand." As we saw earlier, a strong hand is a reference to God's signs and wonders, God's miracles, which refer to the plagues. God knew from the beginning He was going to use force because Pharaoh simply wouldn't comply. Moses wasn't going to compel or persuade Pharaoh by talking him into freeing Israel or even by ordering him to do it. Satan is the same, and so are his oppressing taskmasters. God had to use force to deliver us from Satan's oppression and He has to employ that same power to fulfill that freedom in our walk today. This power is exerted in the form of signs and wonders.

Human oppressors must also be forced to let us go. Criminals certainly require that. Children, likewise, require spanking, not abuse, according to Scripture, to be delivered from becoming oppressors as adults.[60] Abusive spouses require drastic actions, the oppressed spouse needs to remove him or herself from under their direct influence. Do you suffer under an oppressive boss? God may want you to endure a little longer or He may want you remove yourself from that situation, but sooner or later God will deal with that person, even if you never know about it. Romans 12 instructs us not to repay evil with evil, but to leave any vengeance to God. This isn't meant as a wish for God to smack every person that cuts me off on the freeway, or every student that bullies my children. This is a

---

[60] Prov 22:15; 23:13-14; 29:15

mature desire for God to intervene in their lives so that person can be free from the oppression they themselves are under, and by which they oppress others. It's the desire Paul expressed to Timothy:

> 2 Tim 2:25 With gentleness correcting those who are in opposition, if perhaps God may grant them repentance leading to the knowledge of the truth.

4. Oppressors are under oppression

In Exodus 1 Pharaoh saw himself as a victim of Israel, and used that as justification to enslave them and even to murder them.

> Ex 1:8-10 Now a new king arose over Egypt, who did not know Joseph. He said to his people, "Behold, the people of the sons of Israel are more and mightier than we. "Come, let us deal wisely with them, or else they will multiply and in the event of war, they will also join themselves to those who hate us, and fight against us and depart from the land."

That thought would be laughable except it was deadly serious. We don't know if Pharaoh was a mad man or if this was political manipulation, or even both! What we know is that such oppression could've only originated in Satan, Israel's, and God's, sworn enemy. In fact, Satan used the same tactic with Eve in the garden: "You are a victim of God, there are things He's keeping from you. He knows when you eat of the fruit you will be His equal, and He doesn't want that!" No doubt Satan saw Himself as a victim of God too when he decided to seize God's throne and be worshipped by the angels.

King Saul is the case of a hard man who both saw himself as a victim of David, and at the same time was greatly oppressed by Satan because of the spiritual doors he left open in his life. His inability to deal with David's success was compounded by the fears Satan put in his heart, not unlike what Satan did with Pharaoh in Exodus 1. People who see themselves as victims, who are not forgiving of others, are in a prison. This is the case whether the offense was real or perceived. That's what Jesus teaches in His story of the man that was forgiven a large debt but didn't forgive the one who owed him a little.[61] A spiritual prison is where Satan keeps and afflicts an unforgiving person. And even if it is a passive person, in time, there is great probability that they too will become an oppressor, even if just with their words.

5. Oppressors enslave others to themselves

Pharaoh refused to yield to God but continued to hold Israel captive, to keep them under subjection.

> Ex 9:2 "For if you refuse to let *them* go and continue to hold them . . .

Pharaoh "did not let the sons of Israel go out of his land."[62] Satan's desire is to keep people in his "land," people who have been promised a fruitful land, a fruitful life. Satan's land is his soil, which remains dry for lack of rain, full of stones, full of thorns and thistles, producing tares instead of wheat, producing bread of false teaching, full of the beasts of the field, with the lion seeking whom to devour and with the birds of the air stealing the good seed. That's the land Satan wants you to live in as your portion and inheritance. Ultimately, that's what Satan wants to do through human oppressors. That's what he accomplishes through oppressing coaches, child molesters, mean teachers, ungodly church leaders, lustful neighbors, abusive step-parents, etc.

Satan wants you and me not only to live in his "land," but he wants us to toil his land, to serve him.

> Ex 14:5 When the king of Egypt was told that the people had fled . . . they said, "What is this we have done, that we have let Israel go from serving us?"

---

61   Matt 18:23-35
62   Ex 11:10

6. God hardens oppressors by ensnaring them

Let's now tackle a big theological question: Did God harden Pharaoh's heart so he had no choice but to reject God? Let's look into this and then see what we learn from that.

In total, there are three Hebrew words translated "harden" or "hardened," found in the book of Exodus in reference to Pharaoh. The three words are: "chazak" which means "strong;" "kabed" which as we saw earlier means "heavy, unresponsive;" and the last is "kashah" which means "hard." Combined, these words occur 20 times in the context of God's dealings with Pharaoh in Exodus. Ten of those times it is said that God hardened Pharaoh's heart, and in the other ten Pharaoh hardened his own heart. The two following tables help us see every verse under every one of these words, plus some grammatical information we'll discuss below.

God Hardens Pharaoh

Chazak—*piel* (Causative: God acts to bring about a certain condition)	Ex 4:21 but I will harden his heart
	Ex 9:12 And the LORD hardened Pharaoh's heart
	Ex 10:20 But the LORD hardened Pharaoh's heart
	Ex 10:27 But the LORD hardened Pharaoh's heart
	Ex 11:10 the LORD hardened Pharaoh's heart
	Ex 14:4 "Thus I will harden Pharaoh's heart
	Ex 14:8 The LORD hardened the heart of Pharaoh
	Ex 14:17 "I will harden the hearts of the Egyptians
Kabed—*hifil*: (Causative: God causes a certain action to be performed)	Ex 10:1 Then the LORD said to Moses, "Go to Pharaoh, for I have hardened his heart and the heart of his servants

Kashah—*hifil* (Causative: God causes a certain action to be performed)	Ex 7:3 "But I will harden Pharaoh's heart

Here we have all three Hebrew words represented. The words *piel* and *hifil* are Hebrew grammatical categories that tell us the type of action of a verb. In these three cases the action is causative. That means God is causing the condition to come about or causing the action being performed. With the *piel* we have that Pharaoh's heart is in a certain condition: hardened! God acted in such a way that brought about that condition. We will see later what was that action God performed that brought about this condition. With the *hifil* we have that God caused a certain action to be performed. That action was the hardening of the heart. We will see later how God caused that action.

Pharaoh Hardens Himself

Chazak—*kal* (Simple action)	Ex 7:13 Yet Pharaoh's heart was hardened, and he did not listen to them
	Ex 7:22 Pharaoh's heart was hardened, and he did not listen to them
	Ex 8:19 But Pharaoh's heart was hardened, and he did not listen to them
	Ex 9:35 Pharaoh's heart was hardened, and he did not let the sons of Israel go
Kabed—*hifil* (Causative: Pharaoh causes a certain action to be performed)	Ex 8:15 But when Pharaoh saw that there was relief, he hardened his heart and did not listen to them
	Ex 8:32 But Pharaoh hardened his heart this time also, and he did not let the people go
	Ex 9:34 But when Pharaoh saw that the rain and the hail and the thunder had ceased, he sinned again and hardened his heart, he and his servants
Kabed—*kal* (Simple action)	Ex 9:7 But the heart of Pharaoh was hardened, and he did not let the people go
Kabed—Adjective	Ex 7:14 Then the LORD said to Moses, "Pharaoh's heart is stubborn; he refuses to let the people go
Kashah—*hifil* (Causative: Pharaoh causes a certain action to be performed)	Ex 13:15 'It came about, when Pharaoh was stubborn about letting us go . . .

In this second case we have all three Hebrew words as well. We see the verbal categories of *hifil* and a new one, the *kal*, which wasn't present before. We also have one of the words occurring as an adjective. As in the previous table, the *hifil* here is also causative: Pharaoh causes the action to be performed. The *kal* is the basic action, and we'll talk about that shortly. The adjective simply describes Pharaoh's heart as in a certain condition.

Let's now begin to process the information contained in these tables. First, these verses are talking about Pharaoh's heart, primarily his will. When a person's will is hardened that means they are firm and determined in their intention, and nothing will deter them from doing that. See for instance:

> Josh 23:6 Be very firm (*chazak*), then, to keep and do all that is written in the book of the law of Moses, so that you may not turn aside from it to the right hand or to the left

This firm determination means that I will not allow any opposition to deter me from carrying out that which I have decided to do. Joshua was commanded to deal with his fears by making strong his firm resolution.

> Josh 1:9 "Have I not commanded you? Be strong (*chazak*) and courageous! Do not tremble or be dismayed

> Deut 31:6 "Be strong and courageous, do not be afraid or tremble at them

Nothing was supposed to move Joshua's will. His heart was supposed to be hardened, in a positive way, not allowing fear to weaken his determination of carrying out God's commands. The same things are true of Pharaoh, but in a negative way. Pharaoh's heart, his will, was determined to not let Israel go. His will was hard (kashah), it was unmovable (kabed).

In the verses that state Pharaoh hardened himself, under the *kal* action, in every single instance, the heart is the one carrying out the simple action. The heart hardened itself. Pharaoh's will hardened. He did it himself; he made firm his own determination. Under the *hifil*, Pharaoh himself caused the action of hardening. When Pharaoh was confronted with a decision of the will, in light of these plagues and of the obvious sovereignty of the God of Israel, Pharaoh still refused to hear and obey God to let the people go, to humble himself before God (Ex 10:3) and to fear Him (Ex 9:30). Just as Joshua never let fear weaken his resolve to obey God, so Pharaoh never let the fear of God weaken his determination to not yield to the God of Israel. Pharaoh made his will strong, hardened, by repeatedly refusing to yield his will to God. The more Pharaoh rejected God the stronger his resolution to reject Him became.

What does it mean then that God hardened Pharaoh? As we saw earlier, under the *piel* God acted to bring about the hardened condition of Pharaoh's heart. What did God do to bring that about? Under the *hifil* God caused an action to be performed. The action, in context, is the hardening. How did God cause that? The direct answer to this has two parts: God sent a lie that Pharaoh believed, and God continued the same request that was easy for Pharaoh to reject. These two things caused Pharaoh to perform the actions, on his own will, that hardened his heart (believe the lie and reject God), which brought about the condition of being hardened! Biblically speaking, God "ensnared" Pharaoh:

> Ex 10:7 Pharaoh's servants said to him, "How long will this man be a snare to us? Let the men go, that they may serve the LORD their God. Do you not realize that Egypt is destroyed?"

The word "snare" speaks of a trap to catch birds. Figuratively, it refers to an enemy putting a stumbling block. A stumbling block is when God establishes things a certain way and people don't want to conform to it. This becomes a test in which they fail and suffer the consequences of their rejection of God and His ways. Because of his strong rejection of God, Pharaoh opened himself to satanic lies, which he readily believed.

Of the verses in which God hardened Pharaoh, 4 are predictive: God telling Moses ahead of time. Let's examine the context of the other verses.

Pharaoh Hardens Himself	Context and Explanation
Ex 7:13 Yet Pharaoh's heart was hardened, and he did not listen to them	Pharaoh's magicians duplicate the snake sign, so he believes the lie that he doesn't need to fear God
Ex 7:22 Pharaoh's heart was hardened, and he did not listen to them	Pharaoh's magicians duplicate the sign of the water turned into blood, so again he believes the lie that he doesn't need to fear God
Ex 8:15 But when Pharaoh saw that there was relief, he hardened his heart and did not listen to them	This relief emboldened Pharaoh in his rejection of God.
Ex 8:19 But Pharaoh's heart was hardened, and he did not listen to them	Unable to duplicate the gnats, the magicians declared it a work of God, which infuriated Pharaoh, hardening his resolve.
Ex 8:32 But Pharaoh hardened his heart this time also, and he did not let the people go	The relief from the flies was used as a lie by Satan, furthering Pharaoh's hardening.
Ex 9:7 But the heart of Pharaoh was hardened, and he did not let the people go	In the face of undeniable evidence of God's sovereignty (God choosing the onset of this plague, and sparing the Israelites), Pharaoh remained unmoved in his resolve.

God Hardens Pharaoh	Context and Explanation
Ex 9:12 And the LORD hardened Pharaoh's heart, and he did not listen to them, just as the LORD had spoken to Moses.	God placed a stumbling block before Pharaoh by dealing him a severe blow that would require him to humble himself . . . the very thing he would not do.
Ex 9:34 But when Pharaoh saw that the rain and the hail and the thunder had ceased, he sinned again and hardened his heart, he and his servants. Ex 9:35 Pharaoh's heart was hardened, and he did not let the sons of Israel go	Pharaoh faked humility and compassion, but didn't fool Moses or God. He probably thought he obtained a victory, but it was God's ordained deception he believed.
Ex 10:20 But the LORD hardened Pharaoh's heart, and he did not let the sons of Israel go.	Once again, by removing the plague of locust the Lord's relief caused Pharaoh to harden his own heart.
Ex 10:27 But the LORD hardened Pharaoh's heart, and he was not willing to let them go.	The Lord again put a stumbling block before Pharaoh by ordering the total release of Israel, and that showed his utter unwillingness to do that.
Ex 14:8 The LORD hardened the heart of Pharaoh, king of Egypt, and he chased after the sons of Israel as the sons of Israel were going out boldly.	The Lord made it look like Israel was wandering in the desert, and Pharaoh couldn't resist the opportunity, deceitful as it was, to erase his humiliation at God's hand by bringing Israel back to slavery.

Allow me to illustrate what we've said so far. Imagine you are a police officer and I am car thief. You know I'm a bad guy, and you want to catch me, but you can't prove it. Here's what you do: you go undercover. You know my hang out, so you bring a real nice car, park it, leave it running with the keys in and the radio on, and walk into a store. I quickly move in, get in, and drive away. Before I leave the parking lot, 10 of your police buddies descend on me in their undercover cars. You trapped me. You didn't "make me" do it, but you created the conditions upon which I made my own decision. If I would've been a good citizen, a car left running would not have led me to decide to steal it. Likewise, God didn't make Pharaoh do it, to the point that poor Pharaoh had no choice. God simply set up the conditions, Pharaoh made his own decision.

Even in the face of utter defeat at the cross, Satan's hardened heart leads him to attack God and His people, you and me. In the same manner, a person with a hardened heart is deceived and ensnared by God to bring about his much needed humiliation, hopefully leading to true humility, repentance and freedom.

7. The oppressor's first response is to intensify oppression
This is what Pharaoh did:

> Ex 5:9 "Let the labor be heavier on the men, and let them work at it so that they will pay no attention to false words."

This, of course, is exactly what Satan does. He intimidates you, me and whoever stands to gain freedom from oppression and bondage.

8. The oppressor's second response is to bargain for partial freedom
However, when the intimidation is resisted, Satan resorts to working out deals to obtain relief. His intention, though, never changes, so after a person gives in to Satan's bargaining, he hardens his heart and keep him or her under bondage all the same.

Ex 10:11 "Not so! Go now, the men *among you,* and serve the LORD, for that is what you desire."

Ex 8:15 But when Pharaoh saw that there was relief, he hardened his heart and did not listen to them, as the LORD had said.

If Satan can get us to settle for only partial services to God, under a small measure of freedom, he'll call that a victory! Beware of this as you minister freedom to others. If the chains are only partially broken, the links will find a way to "link up" again and keep the person in bondage.

9. Oppressors refuse to submit to authority

When believers minister freedom they may find resistance, a firm will on the part of strongholds and principalities. These may not "listen" at first, like Pharaoh.

Ex 8:19 Then the magicians said to Pharaoh, "This is the finger of God." But Pharaoh's heart was hardened, and he did not listen to them, as the LORD had said.

Ex 5:2 But Pharaoh said, "Who is the LORD that I should obey His voice to let Israel go? I do not know the LORD, and besides, I will not let Israel go."

What brings submission to God's authority is judgment, Jesus' judgment through His death and resurrection that defeated Satan and his hosts and paid for our freedom. The person ministering freedom needs to be submitted to authority. This occurs when he or she applies God's judgment over Satan and the flesh to his or her life.

10. Oppressors feel they are, or should be, superior
This is the essence of why they won't humble and submit themselves before God.

> Ex 9:17 "Still you exalt yourself against My people by not letting them go.

> Ex 10:3 Moses and Aaron went to Pharaoh and said to him, "Thus says the LORD, the God of the Hebrews, 'How long will you refuse to humble yourself before Me? Let My people go, that they may serve Me.

Self-exaltation and pride, which is a refusal to humble oneself, are two sides of the same coin. Even when disguised in false humility. Satan's religiosity can take both forms. It can take the form of a self-exalting, boastful and self-righteous person, but it can also take the form of one blinded to his motives under false humility. The feeling of superiority prevents the person from truly humbling him or herself and letting go of the oppression they bring to others. Superiority is simply acting out the need for self-exaltation. Usually, a self-exalting person, one who acts with superiority, does so because they are under oppression. They live, consciously or not, with deep accusations of worthlessness, often through comparison. These accusations may have originated with people, but are always used by taskmasters. Their boastful ways are simply a defense mechanism by which they hurt others before being hurt again. These dynamics of superiority and worthlessness are often found in superiority because of race, appearance and religiosity.

11. Oppressors use religious accusations
Pharaoh dons his religious garb and takes an oath in the name of the God of Israel, accusing Israel of having evil in their mind!

> Ex 10:10-11 Then he said to them, "Thus may the LORD be with you, if ever I let you and your little

> ones go! Take heed, for evil is in your mind. "Not so!
> Go now, the men *among you,* and serve the LORD,
> for that is what you desire." So they were driven out
> from Pharaoh's presence.

This thought is repulsive, Pharaoh taking an oath in God's name. But such is Satan's religiosity. Satan quoted Scripture to Jesus to cause Him to disobey God! How much more would he try that on us. Religious oppressors accuse people of not being as good as they should be. They often use that as justification for their "lording over" their oppressive religious "exhortations." Much preaching, though "based" on the Word of God, are nothing more than the exhortations of religious people based on accusations and not on compassion. This kind of teaching results in further bondage and condemnation rather than freedom. Instead of coming against the spiritual forces afflicting those they minister to and bringing judgment against those forces of affliction, such teachers, preachers, leaders, counselors, etc., by preaching commandments of men, promote a spirit of slavery rather than a spirit of adoption and freedom.

12. God uses oppressors to defeat oppressors
Let's take the time now to explain this truth and illustrate it in Pharaoh's life.

The staff in Moses' hand, as we saw earlier, stands for demonic activity. The *tsaraat*[63] and the water turned to blood point to death, as does the staff turned into serpent, a figure of Satan and his forces of death. Pharaoh's magicians also had staffs with which they performed their magic, their demonic, counterfeit and deceiving miracles. But the staff in Moses' hand devoured the magicians' staffs, that is, the power of Satan in Moses' hand overcame the power of Satan Pharaoh's servants had. God used Satan to defeat Satan!

---

[63] Translated as "leprosy."

Moses and Aaron used their staffs to introduced most of the plagues. The plagues are demonic activity allowed by God and under His control, much like the way Satan was allowed by God to attack Job. Jesus spoke of this principle when He said:

> Matt 12:25-26 And knowing their thoughts Jesus said to them, "Any kingdom divided against itself is laid waste; and any city or house divided against itself will not stand. "If Satan casts out Satan, he is divided against himself; how then will his kingdom stand?

God used this principle in the natural all throughout the Old Testament confounding Israel's enemies and causing them to fight and kill each other.

> 2 Chr 20:22-23 When they began singing and praising, the LORD set ambushes against the sons of Ammon, Moab and Mount Seir, who had come against Judah; so they were routed. For the sons of Ammon and Moab rose up against the inhabitants of Mount Seir destroying *them* completely; and when they had finished with the inhabitants of Seir, they helped to destroy one another.

Just like God caused Israel's enemies to rise up against each other as a house foolishly divided against each other, so He does with Satan. What seemed as the greatest of Satan's victories, the cross and the grave, became indeed his most utter defeat! God used Satan's ultimate attack on His Son to bring about the ultimate defeat of Satan in the lives of His sons and daughters. The cross and the empty grave are our "staff" with which we apply God's judgment of Satan to minister freedom from bondage to people.

Satan's hardened heart against the freedom of God's people blinds him to the point that he can't discern even when God uses his attacks against himself. Satan is blinded to how God defeats him and has no concern for it.

> Ex 7:22-23 But the magicians of Egypt did the same with their secret arts; and Pharaoh's heart was hardened, and he did not listen to them, as the LORD had said. Then Pharaoh turned and went into his house with no concern even for this.

The practical side of this is that we should not panic when we see Satan attacking us or the people we care about and lead. We can have our eyes and ears open by God to understand and discern that He will use Satan's very attack to judge Satan. The apostle Paul knew this principle in his life.

> 2 Cor 12:7 Because of the surpassing greatness of the revelations, for this reason, to keep me from exalting myself, there was given me a thorn in the flesh, a messenger of Satan to torment me—to keep me from exalting myself!

Note the identity and the purpose of the thorn in the flesh: A messenger (in Greek "angel") of Satan. This was a demon, tormenting Paul (in Greek "strike with the fist"). But God used it to keep Paul from exalting himself, effectively defeating Satan's temptation in Paul's life to be prideful. As a result, this rendered Paul weak through humility, but when he was weak he actually became strong, and that strength was used for the kingdom of God and against Satan's forces. God indeed used Satan to defeat Satan in Paul's life and through him defeat Satan in many people's lives, including yours and mine today.

CHAPTER FOURTEEN

PLAGUES

The staff turned into serpent introduces and defines God's dealings with Pharaoh. But not all the signs and wonders are considered a plague. The staff that became a serpent and the sea that parted and then fell over the Egyptians are not considered plagues. They, nonetheless, were signs and wonders and were carried out with the staff.

> Ex 7:10-12 Aaron threw his staff down before Pharaoh and his servants, and it became a serpent. Then Pharaoh also called for *the* wise men and *the* sorcerers, and they also, the magicians of Egypt, did the same with their secret arts. For each one threw down his staff and they turned into serpents. But Aaron's staff, swallowed up their staffs.

Just as Moses, and more specifically Aaron's staff ate up the magicians' staffs, so God's power was greater than Pharaoh's. This, of course, is a battle between God and Satan, and God is using Satan to defeat Satan. After all, Moses and Aaron's staff turns into a serpent! The satanic power at work in Pharaoh to oppress and afflict Israel was soon to be defeated by God's redemption price paid as judgment to Satan.

Although this was a sign God had given Moses at the burning bush, Aaron was able to perform it because he was acting on behalf of Moses under God's instructions. That's the essence of authority, to operate under submission. The authority to perform signs and wonders, to bring healing and freedom to people from demonic afflictions because of sin and iniquities, comes from being properly submitted. We must be submitted to a leadership that in turn operates under submission. We must be in God's will, both in terms of the church or ministry under which we operate and in terms of what our function is. I must be in submission to God and to His spiritual authority over me. That way the anointing under which my leaders operate will be at my disposal.

The staff's power is the power of death. The staff releases demonic activity over God's opponents, the power of darkness, a certain measure of death, of dying.

> Ps 78:49 He sent upon them His burning anger, fury
> and indignation and trouble, a band of destroying
> angels.

That's exactly what the cross does. Jesus' death, Satan's greatest attack, brought about death to Satan and his forces. It's the most astonishing and ironic reversals of all! Through death, God defeated death. Through the darkest moment in history, God defeated darkness. God used Satan to defeat Satan. He used death to overcome death.

Understanding the plagues helps us realize the nature and extent of Satan's loss at the cross. God brought destruction to Pharaoh to break the oppression by which he was holding Israel in bondage. At the cross, God brought destruction to Satan to break the oppression by which he holds in bondage those to whom you minister.

Let's examine each plague briefly in order to learn about God's destruction of Satan and his taskmasters. Egypt, the oppressor, was overrun, overwhelmed and defeated by evil demons.

"The word plague is borrowed from the Greek *plege*, meaning "blow." Like plague, many of the words for disease and suffering in both Hebrew and Greek, as well as in the surrounding cultures of Mesopotamia and Egypt, derive from the vocabulary of attack and weaponry . . . Consider the similar English terminology, especially the word roots behind plague (flog), affliction, scourge (whip), blight (blow), blast, stroke (strike) and more."[64]

Just as God's anger is tied to "a band of destroying angels," so His anger is manifested through plagues:

> Ps 78:50 He leveled a path for His anger; He did not spare their soul from death, but gave over their life to the plague

The plagues are the work of destructive demons.

1. Blood

The first plague was the turning of all the waters of Egypt into blood.

> Ex 7:20 So Moses and Aaron did even as the LORD had commanded. And he lifted up the staff and struck the water that *was* in the Nile, in the sight of Pharaoh and in the sight of his servants, and all the water that *was* in the Nile was turned to blood.

The Nile's seasonal flooding irrigated Egypt's agricultural lands. The Egyptians considered the flooded Nile as a god of fertility. Therefore, turning the Nile into blood affected Egypt's agriculture and was a blow to their gods. Particularly, the attack on the false gods was a mockery and humiliation. This shows the foolishness of trusting in idols that can't control nature. In attacking the Egyptian gods the

---

[64] Dictionary of Biblical Imagery, s.v. "Plague," 648.

Lord really is defeating Satan and his oppressors. Let's see how this defeat in the physical realm translates into the spiritual.

The bleeding Nile is the picture of a corpse, incapable of anything. The effects of this are: 1. Mockery, humiliation and ironic reversal; 2. Agricultural failure; 3. Thirst; 4. Torment from the repulsive stench.

Through this we learn how God defeats the enemy: 1. God turns Satan's intent into the opposite, an ironic reversal, confusion in his camp; 2. He brings failure to demonic seeds in our lives, Satan's lies, so they don't become fruitful; 3. Jesus sends demons to waterless places, thirsty wilderness, where they find unfruitfulness; 4. Just as the instrument of fertility became a tormenting stench, so Satan's failed plans bring torment to his demons.

Let's see how this plague is a pattern of redemption in Scripture.

> Rev 16:3-7 The second angel poured out his bowl into the sea, and it became blood like that of a dead man; and every living thing in the sea died. Then the third angel poured out his bowl into the rivers and the springs of waters; and they became blood. And I heard the angel of the waters saying, "Righteous are You, who are and who were, O Holy One, because You judged these things; for they poured out the blood of saints and prophets, and You have given them blood to drink. They deserve it." And I heard the altar saying, "Yes, O Lord God, the Almighty, true and righteous are Your judgments."

The waters are turned to blood as a result of the bowls of God's wrath. God's wrath, as we saw in David's life, is demonic activity. This is the same as the instrument God used to turn the waters into blood in Egypt: Moses' staff, which was the power of demonic activity. In verses 5 to 7 the prevailing thought is that turning the waters into blood is a righteous judgment for oppressing the saints, an ironic reversal for spilling their blood. The same theme of righteous judgment to the oppressors is present in Exodus.

God's judgment is a compassionate decision to release the oppressed from the power of the oppressor, by pouring out demonic activity on the oppressor. God's wrath was poured out on Satan at Jesus' death and resurrection. What we do today is to skillfully apply that defeat to Satan and his angels. Knowing this deeply in our hearts increases our confident authority that He is already victorious as we minister to people oppressed by Satan.

2. Frogs

With the Nile still flooded God brought the second plague.

> Ex 8:2-4 "But if you refuse to let them go, behold, I will smite your whole territory with frogs. "The Nile will swarm with frogs, which will come up and go into your house and into your bedroom and on your bed, and into the houses of your servants and on your people, and into your ovens and into your kneading bowls. "So the frogs will come up on you and your people and all your servants.""'"

The ponds formed by the flooded Nile produced frogs every year in Egypt. For the Egyptians the frog was also a sign of fertility, and even of resurrection. There were gods associated with this.

This plague features some of the same ideas as the previous one: mockery and humiliation of Egyptian gods, fertility failure, torment and stench. We see that the frogs constitute a very personal attack: in Pharaoh's bed, kitchen utensils, etc. This is repulsive, frustrating and enraging. But there's nothing Pharaoh can do against this God-inflicted frustration. The same is true with Satan and his demons.

This plague, however, has a deeper side to it.

> Rev 16:13-14 And I saw coming out of the mouth
> of the dragon and out of the mouth of the beast and
> out of the mouth of the false prophet, three unclean
> spirits like frogs; for they are spirits of demons,
> performing signs, which go out to the kings of the
> whole world, to gather them together for the war of
> the great day of God, the Almighty.

The frogs that attacked Egypt were demonic. God uses demonic activity to oppress and defeat demonic oppressors. According to Revelation 16 frogs represent demons with powerful lies. The lies cause many demons to gather against God. But God is in control. He gathers them in order to defeat them.

God does the same in the lives of people. When you see increased demonic activity be aware that God has gathered them in order to defeat them. A word of knowledge would reveal to you the nature of the activity. A word of wisdom would reveal to you how God wants you to deliver the person from oppression.

3. Gnats
Let's consider now the third plague.

> Ex 8:16-17 Then the LORD said to Moses, "Say to
> Aaron, 'Stretch out your staff and strike the dust of
> the earth, that it may become gnats through all the
> land of Egypt.'" They did so; and Aaron stretched
> out his hand with his staff, and struck the dust of
> the earth, and there were gnats on man and beast.
> All the dust of the earth became gnats through all
> the land of Egypt.

> Ex 8:19 Then the magicians said to Pharaoh, "This
> is the finger of God."

"All the dust of the earth" is a hyperbolic statement to convey the overwhelming intensity of this plague. One of the most likely gnats referred to here was a stinging gnat. Those two facts combined constitute a tormenting nightmare of a plague.

The dust of the earth speaks of three things. First, it speaks of dry soil, a wilderness. The gnats represent an overwhelming failure of Satan's purposes. Second, dust speaks of death, a return to dust. And third, dust represents the serpent's humiliation and curse. Just as God paralyzed Egypt and halted the success of their oppression, so He does to Satan's spiritual oppressors.

Pharaoh's own servants admitted this plague was the finger of God. As we saw earlier, Jesus taught that the Finger of God is a Person:

> Luke 11:20 "But if I cast out demons by the finger of God, then the kingdom of God has come upon you.

> Matt. 12:28 "But if I cast out demons by the Spirit of God, then the kingdom of God has come upon you.

According to this, the kingdom of God comes when, by the Holy Spirit, Jesus frees people by supernaturally defeating the demonic activity that oppresses them. These are the signs and wonders Jesus did, the same God did through Moses and Aaron, and the same He's given us authority to perform. The Holy Spirit has anointed us to bring healing and freedom to people by the signs and wonders of supernatural judgment on spiritual oppressors.

4. Flies
The fourth plague, the plague of flies, has several things in common with the previous plague, the plague of gnats.

Ex 8:23-24 "I will put a division between My people and your people. And there came great swarms of flies into the house of Pharaoh and the houses of his servants and the land was laid waste because of the swarms of flies in all the land of Egypt.

Psa 78:45 He sent among them swarms of flies which devoured them,

Just as the gnats stung the Egyptians, so the flies bit them. The Hebrew word translated "devoured" in Psalm 78 is the normal word for eating, and it is used metaphorically of how a fire consumes. In other words, in Hebrew, a fire devours. This fly was a devourer, and its bite burnt. God's judgment devours Satan's forces.

The flies came in swarms, great swarms. The word translated "great" is a word we've seen before, "kaved," and it means heavy. The heaviness and devouring of these swarms of flies made them a torment of overwhelming intensity.

The demons are associated with flies. The name Beelzebul, which means "lord of flies," is a designation for Satan, ruler of demons. God sent swarms of demons to defeat the oppressors and free His people.

Not surprisingly, these flies in Egypt caused blindness. Likewise demons, in their blindness, can't see how their attacks are the very ways God brings their defeat.

Finally, God put "a division" between Israel and the Egyptians. The word translated "division" means redemption. God put a redemption between His people and the oppressors. What does that mean? Redemption, as we've seen before, is the payment of freedom's price. This payment is judgment over the oppressor to free the oppressed. God put over Pharaoh's people the judgment that would free His people. When God defeats the oppressors in our lives, He puts His judgments on them, not on us, and set us free.

5. Pestilence

This plague, pestilence, was also a "heavy" plague.

> Ex 9:2-5 "For if you refuse to let them go and continue to hold them, behold, the hand of the LORD will come with a very severe pestilence on your livestock which are in the field, on the horses, on the donkeys, on the camels, on the herds, and on the flocks. "But the LORD will make a distinction between the livestock of Israel and the livestock of Egypt, so that nothing will die of all that belongs to the sons of Israel.""

The word "kaved" is used in verse 3 where it is translated as "severe," and it speaks again of this plague's overwhelming intensity. In none of these heavy plagues is there a report of death. God didn't destroy Egypt completely in order to keep displaying His nature to the world. He does the same against Satan and his forces. God uses pestilence on oppressors who refuse to let people go free.

> Jer 34:17 "Therefore thus says the LORD, 'You have not obeyed Me in proclaiming release each man to his brother and each man to his neighbor. Behold, I am proclaiming a release to you,' declares the LORD, 'to the sword, to the pestilence and to the famine; and I will make you a terror to all the kingdoms of the earth.

The destruction that pestilence can have is shown in the following passage.

> 2 Sam 24:15 So the LORD sent a pestilence upon Israel from the morning until the appointed time,

and seventy thousand men of the people from Dan
to Beersheba died.[65]

By striking the livestock of Egypt at least two things were
accomplished. First, a mockery and humiliation of the god's of
Egypt (bulls and cows). And second, Egypt's economy was further
decimated.

God sent pestilence, a severe, decimating disease, over the oppressors
but spared the oppressed. God judges sin in our lives in order to
set us free from bondage. He applies the judgment of the cross to
spiritual bondage.

6. Boils

The next plague, boils, attacked animals like pestilence did, but
people also suffered under it.

> Ex 9:8-9 Then the LORD said to Moses and Aaron,
> "Take for yourselves handfuls of soot from a kiln,
> and let Moses throw it toward the sky in the sight
> of Pharaoh. "It will become fine dust over all the
> land of Egypt, and will become boils breaking out
> with sores on man and beast through all the land
> of Egypt."

> Ex 9:11 The magicians could not stand before
> Moses because of the boils, for the boils were on
> the magicians as well as on all the Egyptians.

A well known Bible case of a person with boils is Job. The Hebrew
word for boils used in Exodus 9 is the same used of Job.

---

[65] The morning probably refers to 6:00 am when the lighted part of the day
began to be counted. There were two daily appointed times, one at 9:00
am and the other at 3:00 pm. This pestilence lasted from 6:00 am to 9:00
am, 3 hours, or from 6:00 am to 3:00 pm, 6 hours. In either case, that's
70,000 people in less than half a day!

Job 2:7 Then Satan went out from the presence of
the LORD and smote Job with sore boils from the
sole of his foot to the crown of his head.

A much greater victory and fruitfulness came to Job when God
defeated Satan's most vicious attack in his life. Just as Job was
tormented by the boils, so were the Egyptians, and so are the demonic
forces when we apply God's defeat over them on the cross.

Boils form when the skin is burnt. A kiln is a brick oven, and the soot
is burnt residue from the kiln. Putting all this together we have that
God turn the fiery oppression of brick making on the Egyptians.
The oppressors were now suffering oppression. When you minister
to people who are oppressed be confident that God, on the authority
of the cross and resurrection of Jesus, will bring torment back on
the oppressors.

7. Hail

Hail is a form of precipitation. In Scripture we have rain, flood, hail,
and fire and brimstone. Of all these, only rain is beneficial, the rest
are progressively destructive.

Ex 9:18 "Behold, about this time tomorrow, I will
send a very heavy hail, such as has not been seen in
Egypt from the day it was founded until now.

Ex 9:20 The one among the servants of Pharaoh who
feared the word of the LORD made his servants and
his livestock flee into the houses;

Ex 9:23 Moses stretched out his staff toward the
sky, and the LORD sent thunder and hail, and fire
ran down to the earth. And the LORD rained hail
on the land of Egypt.

> Ex 9:25 The hail struck all that was in the field
> through all the land of Egypt, both man and beast;
> the hail also struck every plant of the field and
> shattered every tree of the field.

The two most famous precipitations in the Bible are Noah's flood and the fire and brimstone that destroyed Sodom and Gomorrah. The "heavy" (kaved) hail caused severe damage to agriculture, and killed beasts and people. This was a mockery and humiliation of Egypt's deities of sky and crops.

As in previous plagues, God targeted the oppressor but spared His people.

> Ex 9:26 Only in the land of Goshen, where the sons
> of Israel were, there was no hail.

The text offers details that help us date this plague:

> Ex 9:31 (Now the flax and the barley were ruined,
> for the barley was in the ear and the flax was in
> bud. But the wheat and the spelt were not ruined,
> for they ripen late.)

The hail took place before the barley was harvested, which means sometime around late January or early February. Barley speaks of bread. Flax was used in Egypt as fabric to create linen clothing, which was characteristically how their priests dressed. Egyptians did not favor wool clothing.

Psalm 78 gives further detail about this plague:

> Psa 78:47-49 He destroyed their vines with hailstones
> and their sycamore trees with frost. He gave over
> their cattle also to the hailstones and their herds to
> bolts of lightning. He sent upon them His burning

anger, fury and indignation and trouble, a band of destroying angels.

The hail didn't just destroyed Egypt's Spring crops (barley and flax), it also destroyed their Summer fruits (vines and sycamore). Watch now the spiritual side of this: God's anger, fury, indignation and trouble were actually demons. The Psalmist calls them "a band of destroying angles." Hail represents demonic activity. As we saw earlier, the anger of the Lord is Satan himself. God turns Satan's house against itself. The demonic activity of the hail destroyed Pharaoh's bread (barley), and rejoicing (vines).

Demons disguise as angles of light. Angels dress in fine linen. The Egyptian priests were Satan's agents, a counterfeit of ministers of light. When God destroyed the flax He was showing how He destroys demonic disguises. Demons primarily disguise behind partial truths, which are nothing but lies. God's hail destroys the strongholds, the refuges of lies

> Is 28:17 "I will make justice the measuring line and righteousness the level; then hail will sweep away the refuge of lies and the waters will overflow the secret place.

8. Locust

Locust is perhaps the plague easiest to see as demonic activity in the Bible.

> Ex 10:12-17 Then the LORD said to Moses, "Stretch out your hand over the land of Egypt for the locusts, that they may come up on the land of Egypt and eat every plant of the land, even all that the hail has left." So Moses stretched out his staff over the land of Egypt, and the LORD directed an east wind on the land all that day and all that night; and when it was morning, the east wind brought

the locusts. The locusts came up over all the land of Egypt and settled in all the territory of Egypt; they were very numerous. There had never been so many locusts, nor would there be so many again. For they covered the surface of the whole land, so that the land was darkened; and they ate every plant of the land and all the fruit of the trees that the hail had left. Thus nothing green was left on tree or plant of the field through all the land of Egypt. Then Pharaoh hurriedly called for Moses and Aaron, and he said, "I have sinned against the LORD your God and against you. "Now therefore, please forgive my sin only this once, and make supplication to the LORD your God, that He would only remove this death from me."

Ex 10:19 So the LORD shifted the wind to a very strong west wind which took up the locusts and drove them into the Red Sea; not one locust was left in all the territory of Egypt.

Again, the Egyptians found themselves overwhelmed under the incredible amount of locusts that came on them overnight. The sights and sounds must have been terrifying to all. With all this, no report of deaths is found in the text. God "made a mockery of the Egyptians."[66]

The Dictionary of Biblical Imagery says:

"The sheer numbers of locusts in a swarm (Judg 6:5; 7:12; Jer 46:23; 51:14), the physical resemblance of their heads to horses' heads (Job 39:20; Jer 51:27; Rev 9:7), their unbroken advance (Prov 30:27), their ability to "strip the land" (Nahum 3:15-17) and their thunderous

---

[66]   Ex 10:2

approach (Rev 9:9) make a plague of locusts a suitable metaphor for an invading army.

"The prophecy of Joel was occasioned by an invasion of locusts (Joel 2:1-11, 25), which in Joel's prophetic imagination became an emblem of divine judgment against an apostate nation. Joel describes the invasion with minute and technical accuracy, referring, for example, to "the cutting locust," "the swarming locust," "the hopping locust" and "the destroying locust" (Joel 1:4 RSV) in reference to the stages of the locusts' development. Joel compares the sight and sound of a plague of locusts to "a powerful army drawn up for battle" (Joel 2:5 RSV). The locusts approach like a black cloud or a spreading dawn (Joel 2:2). On closer inspection they look and sound like galloping cavalry (Joel 2:4), advancing like trained soldiers who march in line, not swerving from their course (Joel 2:7). Their beating wings and chomping mouths crackle like a great fire (Joel 2:5), and like a fire they devour everything in their path (Joel 2:3; cf. 1:4)."[67]

Israel was spared from the hail, but apparently they were not spared from the locust. First, the text doesn't say specifically that God made a distinction between them and Egypt. And second, the text emphatically says several times that the locust covered all the land of Egypt. God didn't bring judgment on Israel, rather, God finished off Egypt's economy, agriculture, so they couldn't even go to Goshen and salvage any crops. God left Egypt without bread. He brought a famine to them.

God brought the locust to Egypt with an east wind. The Anchor Yale Bible Dictionary has this to say about the east wind:

"The east wind was the wind coming from the desert regions of Syria and Arabia. This east wind is today called a khamsin (literally, "fifty," for it often lasts about fifty days) or sirocco. It comes in a season marked by low humidity, high winds, and extremely hot weather.

---

[67]   Dictionary of Biblical Imagery, s.v. "Locust," 516.

Because the winds come from the desert regions and are strong, they often carry a great deal of dust and sand. Such winds were extremely sultry, causing plants to wither, even stripping fruit from plants and scattering everything in its path. This east wind can be called "the wind of [the LORD]," for he controls it. He uses the east wind as an instrument of his judgment."[68]

We have great depth of meaning here. Let's work through it.

God makes a mockery of Satan by reversing his attacks in ironic ways, setting people free. Even as Israel suffered loss of crops by not being spared in the locust plague, God delivered them from farming and storing Pharaoh's bread. God delivers His people from laboring as slaves to store Satan's "bread," his teachings, his lies. That loss is no loss at all! In fact, God promises to restore the years the locusts have eaten. That is accomplished by remarkable fruitfulness. God restores people from famine by giving them in one year a crop worth two years. God restored double to Job through remarkable fruitfulness. That's what He wants to do for you and those under your influence.

Revelations 9 explains that the locusts really are demons, and it reveals the nature of their spiritual attacks.

> Rev 9:1-6 Then the fifth angel sounded, and I saw a star from heaven which had fallen to the earth; and the key of the bottomless pit was given to him. He opened the bottomless pit, and smoke went up out of the pit, like the smoke of a great furnace; and the sun and the air were darkened by the smoke of the pit. Then out of the smoke came locusts upon the earth, and power was given them, as the scorpions of the earth have power. They were told not to hurt the grass of the earth, nor any green thing, nor

---

68 AYBD, s.v. "EAST," 3:248.

any tree, but only the men who do not have the seal of God on their foreheads. And they were not permitted to kill anyone, but to torment for five months; and their torment was like the torment of a scorpion when it stings a man. And in those days men will seek death and will not find it; they will long to die, and death flees from them.

The locusts show in the natural the true spiritual condition of people, namely, that they aren't fruitful. God judges Satan in their lives so they would repent and receive God's seal, which is Spirit-baptism. These men were hostile to God and His people, oppressors used by Satan, and so they represent demons. Anyone who is an oppressor is enslaving others and is feeding others Satan's bread, his lies. Just as scorpions paralyze their prey with venom, so locusts paralyze oppressors with famine. Just as scorpions devour their paralyzed victims, so famine forced oppressors into slavery. These are all aspects of demonic oppression, both on men and on demons. God uses locusts, scorpions, to defeat oppressors and set people free.

The Hebrew word translated wind is the same word translated spirit. The same is true in the Greek language of the New Testament. The wind that brought the locust represents spiritual forces. In addition, going east represents going out of God's presence. The entrance to the temple, the tabernacle and even the garden of Eden, all look to the east. That means that going out of God's presence one traveled east. To come from the east then is to have a point of origin far from God. Indeed this wind comes from the desert, unfruitfulness. The east wind is demonic activity manifested in the physical, but representing spiritual realities.

We will say more about the east wind, but for now look at a couple of verses:

Hosea 12:1, 15 Ephraim feeds on wind, and pursues the east wind continually; he multiplies lies and

> violence . . . Though he flourishes among the reeds,
> an east wind will come, the wind of the LORD
> coming up from the wilderness; and his fountain
> will become dry and his spring will be dried up; it
> will plunder his treasury of every precious article.

The east wind is a Satanic attack consisting of multiple lies and great oppression, violence. It brings an unfruitful wilderness, drought and famine. On the cross, God turned on Satan this same attack he carried out on the Son of God. Through Jesus' victory God brings the same kind of defeat on the spiritual forces that oppress people.

9. Darkness
The ninth plague, darkness affected Egypt but not the children of Israel.

> Ex 10:21-23 Then the LORD said to Moses, "Stretch
> out your hand toward the sky, that there may be
> darkness over the land of Egypt, even a darkness
> which may be felt." So Moses stretched out his hand
> toward the sky, and there was thick darkness in all
> the land of Egypt for three days. They did not see
> one another, nor did anyone rise from his place for
> three days, but all the sons of Israel had light in
> their dwellings.

This plague was a direct hit to Egypt's main god, the sun-god. This god was a counterfeit of the true God, the Father of light. "Thick darkness" has been translated as *"Darkness of obscurity,* i.e., the deepest darkness. The combination of two words or synonyms gives the greatest intensity to the thought."[69]

---

[69]   C. F. Keil and Delitzsch F., Commentary on the Old Testament, Accordance electronic ed. (Peabody: Hendrickson Publishers, 1996), n.p. [Italics theirs.]

Obviously, darkness speaks of spiritual darkness, of demonic activity that covers the light and leaves people paralyzed.

Darkness also stands for blindness, which speaks of confusion. Notice in the following passages the relationship between blindness and bewilderment.

> Deut 28:28 "The LORD will smite you with madness and with blindness and with bewilderment of heart;

> Zech 12:4 "In that day," declares the LORD, "I will strike every horse with bewilderment and his rider with madness. But I will watch over the house of Judah, while I strike every horse of the peoples with blindness.

Most commentators associate this darkness with the dust clouds of the east wind. This also explains how the darkness was so thick that it could be felt. I have seen pictures of these dust storms in the Middle-East and the biblical description fits perfectly. Huge dust clouds like fog cover the sun. Darkness and dust shut down people in their homes.

Revelations also speak of the effect of the kingdom of darkness.

> Rev 16:10-11 Then the fifth angel poured out his bowl on the throne of the beast, and his kingdom became darkened; and they gnawed their tongues because of pain, and they blasphemed the God of heaven because of their pains and their sores; and they did not repent of their deeds.

Just as darkness fell over Pharaoh and his kingdom, so God sends darkness, confusion, to Satan and his kingdom. By attacking the oppressors this way God brings about liberty to the oppressed.

10. Death of the firstborn

We come now to the last plague. This is the only plague aimed directly to bring about death to the Egyptians, but even then the deaths are kept to a minimum. They are a strategic blow. This plague, however, shares common elements of all the previous ones: a mockery to Egyptian gods, an ironic reversal of Egyptian oppression, a strike against their fruitfulness and an overwhelming torment.

> Ex 11:4-7 Moses said, "Thus says the LORD, 'About midnight I am going out into the midst of Egypt, and all the firstborn in the land of Egypt shall die, from the firstborn of the Pharaoh who sits on his throne, even to the firstborn of the slave girl who is behind the millstones; all the firstborn of the cattle as well. 'Moreover, there shall be a great cry in all the land of Egypt, such as there has not been before and such as shall never be again. 'But against any of the sons of Israel a dog will not even bark, whether against man or beast, that you may understand how the LORD makes a distinction between Egypt and Israel.'

> Ex 12:12-13 'For I will go through the land of Egypt on that night, and will strike down all the firstborn in the land of Egypt, both man and beast; and against all the gods of Egypt I will execute judgments—I am the LORD. 'The blood shall be a sign for you on the houses where you live; and when I see the blood I will pass over you, and no plague will befall you to destroy you when I strike the land of Egypt.

> Ex 12:23 "For the LORD will pass through to smite the Egyptians; and when He sees the blood on the lintel and on the two doorposts, the LORD will

pass over the door and will not allow the destroyer
to come in to your houses to smite you.

Pharaoh was considered a god, and so was his son, specifically
his firstborn son. Behind every god and idol is a demon. Pharaoh
represents Satan himself, the leader of the oppressors. God judged
the gods of Egypt, including Pharaoh. Judgment is the price paid
the oppressor to free the oppressed. The destroyer carried out God's
judgment. God uses Satan to defeat Satan.

The firstborn speaks of the strength of reproduction, fruitfulness.
Pharaoh attacked God's firstborn, Israel, so in an ironic reversal God
now attacks Pharaoh's firstborn. The cry of the Egyptians shows the
acute pain and torment inflicted by God. It would take this much
pain for Egypt to let go of their oppression over Israel.

The sentence "But against any of the sons of Israel a dog will not
even bark" may sound of little meaning, but there's no idle word in
Scripture. The English word "bark" translates two Hebrew words
with the meaning of "to sharpen the tongue." Obviously, the dog
here stands for the destroyer. When God judges the destroying
forces in people's lives He protects the oppressed. A sharp tongue
has to do with threats, words that paint a future of pain, oppression,
intimidation, mental agony and unfruitfulness. In other words,
curses, lies enabled only by agreeing with them. But over those
infused with life, with the blood of the Lamb, demons don't even
speak.

Egypt let Israel go forced by the overwhelming pain of God's plagues.
This set the stage for the final showdown: the crossing of the sea.

CHAPTER FIFTEEN

SEA

THE CROSSING OF THE SEA

The crossing of the sea is the number one experience to which the Old Testament keeps looking back. It is a pattern of how God redeems people: He judges the oppressors setting captives free. References to the arm and the hand of the Lord, to His wonders and miracles, and many others, all point back to this. The traditional synagogue liturgy, to this day, captures the Scriptural priority of this event and makes it a salient point of its weekly celebration and remembrance. God ordered a yearly feast, Passover, for the purpose of remembering all the events connected to the exodus from Egypt.

Just as the earthly tabernacle was patterned after the heavenly original, so this earthly liberating act is patterned after the heavenly and eternal liberating act: Jesus' defeat of Satan. The cross and the resurrection are the pattern, the exodus is the copy. The exodus helps us understand what went on at the cross and the resurrection. So intentional is this pattern that both events, the exodus and the cross, took place on the same day in God's prophetic calendar.

> Ex 14:1-4 Now the LORD spoke to Moses, saying, "Tell the sons of Israel to turn back and camp before Pi-hahiroth, between Migdol and the sea; you shall camp in front of Baal-zephon, opposite it, by the

sea. "For Pharaoh will say of the sons of Israel, 'They are wandering aimlessly in the land; the wilderness has shut them in.' "Thus I will harden Pharaoh's heart, and he will chase after them; and I will be honored through Pharaoh and all his army, and the Egyptians will know that I am the LORD." And they did so.

God made it easy for Pharaoh to show his true colors, that he was an oppressor to the core. Israel carried out God's directions of turning back and camping. Logic would dictate that Israel run as fast as possible for fear that Pharaoh would chase and catch up. Turning back speaks of repentance; camping speaks of remaining, persevering. Those are God's instructions. God had a plan. Likewise, He has a plan to defeat those who oppress us once and for all.

Ex 14:15-16 Then the LORD said to Moses, "Why are you crying out to Me? Tell the sons of Israel to go forward. "As for you, lift up your **staff** and stretch out your hand over the sea and **divide** it, and the sons of Israel shall go through the midst of the sea on **dry** land.[70]

Ex 14:21 Then Moses stretched out his hand over the sea; and the LORD swept the sea back by a strong east wind all night and turned the sea into dry land, so the waters were divided.

With the staff, the instrument of God's signs and wonders, Moses would divide the waters. The division of the waters would bring out the dry land. Once Moses stretched out the staff in his hand over the waters, God divided the waters. How did He do it? By a strong east wind. The Hebrew word for wind is "ruach," and it also means "spirit."

---

[70] Emphasis added.

This is exactly what God did at creation. The Spirit ("Ruach") of God, the Finger of God through whom Jesus performed His kingdom miracles, was moving above the waters. When God gave the word, the Spirit divided the waters and dry land appeared. Although Exodus 14 is a passage of judgment, Genesis 1 is not. These two stories connect and depart at the same point. In Genesis 1 the Spirit of God divides the waters to make the land fruitful, life giving. In Exodus 14 a spirit from the east (not from God), divides the waters to bring about death (to the Egyptians). Ironically, God used this spirit's death-giving action to drown His enemies and bring about redemption to His people. On the cross, Satan brought about death in order to "drown" the Son of God. God, however, raised Him from His burial, represented by water immersion in Romans 6, drowning Satan instead, and redeeming His people. The greatest of all ironic reversals!

The same dynamic is present in Noah's flood. The agent of God's anger, Satan, brought about a flood that made the land unfruitful again. But ironically, through that oppressive process, God destroyed His enemies and saved His people. Noah "walked" on the waters of judgment, much like Peter walked on waters under windy (spirits) conditions.[71] God sent a wind from His presence to once again uncover the dry land to make it fruitful. God defeats floods of iniquities in people's lives by drowning the oppressors and resurrecting people with Christ out of slavery and into fullness of life!

> Ex 14:26-28 Then the LORD said to Moses, "Stretch out your hand over the sea so that the waters may come back over the Egyptians, over their chariots and their horsemen." So Moses stretched out his hand over the sea, and the sea returned to its normal state at daybreak, while the Egyptians were fleeing right into it; then the LORD

---

71 Matt 14:22-33. Study this passage and let God teach you about the wind, doubt and walking over spiritual attacks.

overthrew the Egyptians in the midst of the sea. The waters returned and covered the chariots and the horsemen, even Pharaoh's entire army that had gone into the sea after them; not even one of them remained.

Ex 14:30 Thus the LORD saved Israel that day from the hand of the Egyptians, and Israel saw the Egyptians dead on the seashore.

Based on this passage, Jewish tradition teaches us never to rejoice at our enemies' fall. The Egyptians here represent the forces of oppression, Satan's demons. This passage speaks of Jesus' defeat of Satan. Scripture is very clear about addressing satanic forces:

Jude 8-10 Yet in the same way these men, also by dreaming, defile the flesh, and reject authority, and revile angelic majesties. But Michael the archangel, when he disputed with the devil and argued about the body of Moses, did not dare pronounce against him a railing judgment, but said, "The Lord rebuke you!" But these men revile the things which they do not understand . . .

Although Michael has great authority, has never fallen and is fully aware of Jesus' victory over Satan, he was careful in how he addressed Satan. Michael "did not dare pronounce against him a railing judgment." The word "railing" is a translation of the Greek word "blasphemias," from which we get "blaspheme." This same Greek word is translated as "revile" in verse 10. Jude is warning about the wrong way of doing spiritual warfare. The Greek word "blasphemias" means, "to speak in a disrespectful way that demeans, denigrates."[72] This includes the words said and the way it is said. Jude gives the key to the heart of the people he's describing when he

---

[72]   BDAG, s.v. "blasfemeo," 178.

says that they "reject authority." Look at the following example of this in the natural.

> Acts 23:2-5 The high priest Ananias commanded those standing beside him to strike him on the mouth. Then Paul said to him, "God is going to strike you, you whitewashed wall! Do you sit to try me according to the Law, and in violation of the Law order me to be struck?" But the bystanders said, "Do you revile God's high priest?" And Paul said, "I was not aware, brethren, that he was high priest; for it is written, 'YOU SHALL NOT SPEAK EVIL OF A RULER OF YOUR PEOPLE.'"

Although the word "revile" in verse 4 isn't the same Greek word used by Jude, it is a synonym. Paul spoke disrespectfully to a man in high authority. But the moment Paul became aware that what he had done was wrong, he immediately repented from it. That's the same we should do if indeed we have addressed Satan and his forces in ways inappropriate. To continue doing this opens the person to spiritual defeat due to the legal right conceded by rejecting authority.

> Eccl 10:20 Furthermore, in your bedchamber do not curse a king, and in your sleeping rooms do not curse a rich man, for a bird of the heavens will carry the sound and the winged creature will make the matter known.

The birds of the heavens, as Jesus taught in Matthew 13, represent demons. In the spirit realm it will be known that the person rejects authority. The key to great faith, faith that God honors with miracles, healing and victory, is submission to authority. That's what Jesus taught in His encounter with the Roman centurion in Matthew 8. One of the reasons we don't experience miracles, healings and victory, all for which Christ already died, and for which the Spirit empowers us, could be the way we do spiritual warfare.

Exodus 15 is a fitting conclusion to this section of the book. Please read it in light of all we've learned so far.

Ex 15:1-18 Then Moses and the sons of Israel
sang this song to the LORD, and said,
"I will sing to the LORD, for He is highly exalted;
The horse and its rider He has hurled into the sea.
"The LORD is my strength and song,
And He has become my salvation;
This is my God, and I will praise Him;
My father's God, and I will extol Him.
"The LORD is a warrior;
The LORD is His name.
"Pharaoh's chariots and his army He has cast into the sea;
And the choicest of his officers are drowned in the Red Sea.
"The deeps cover them;
They went down into the depths like a stone.
"Your right hand, O LORD, is majestic in power,
Your right hand, O LORD, shatters the enemy.
"And in the greatness of Your excellence
You overthrow those who rise up against You;
You send forth Your burning anger,
and it consumes them as chaff.
"At the blast of Your nostrils the waters were piled up,
The flowing waters stood up like a heap;
The deeps were congealed in the heart of the sea.
"The enemy said, 'I will pursue, I will overtake,
I will divide the spoil;
My desire shall be gratified against them;
I will draw out my sword, my hand will destroy them.'
"You blew with Your wind, the sea covered them;
They sank like lead in the mighty waters.
"Who is like You among the gods, O LORD?
Who is like You, majestic in holiness,
Awesome in praises, working wonders?
"You stretched out Your right hand,

The earth swallowed them.
"In Your lovingkindness
You have led the people whom You have redeemed;
In Your strength
You have guided them to Your holy habitation.
"The peoples have heard, they tremble;
Anguish has gripped the inhabitants of Philistia.
"Then the chiefs of Edom were dismayed;
The leaders of Moab, trembling grips them;
All the inhabitants of Canaan have melted away.
"Terror and dread fall upon them;
By the greatness of Your arm they are motionless as stone;
Until Your people pass over, O LORD,
Until the people pass over whom You have purchased.
"You will bring them and plant them
in the mountain of Your inheritance,
The place, O LORD,
Which You have made for Your dwelling,
The sanctuary, O Lord, which Your hands have established.
"The LORD shall reign forever and ever.

PART III

BIBLICAL CASE STUDY

CHAPTER SIXTEEN

HOW TO OVERCOME AN UNFRUITFUL HEART

Ruth 1:1-6 Now it came about in the days when the judges governed, that there was a famine in the land. And a certain man of Bethlehem in Judah went to sojourn in the land of Moab with his wife and his two sons. The name of the man was Elimelech, and the name of his wife, Naomi; and the names of his two sons were Mahlon and Chilion, Ephrathites of Bethlehem in Judah. Now they entered the land of Moab and remained there.

The condition of our heart spills over into our walk. We identify the condition of the heart by the walk of the person.

Allow me to re-translate verse one the way it reads literally in Hebrew. It's going to be awkward; it's not going to be good English grammar. I'm going to give you the word order the way it comes in Hebrew because that is important. It says,

> And walked a man from House of Bread (Bethlehem) in Judah, to live as foreigner in the fields of Moab, he with his wife and two sons.

Catch the beginning, "And walked a man from . . ."

1. Elimelech's walk

The focus is on Elimelech's walk. The word "went" is the regular Hebrew word for our spiritual walk. It isn't just that he moved from one place to another, but it's his walk. His heart. Physically, this man's walk is a descent. Walking from Bethlehem to Moab requires that you go down in altitude. He's not going up. That's also true spiritually. Let's take a look at where he is falling from and where is he headed.

Elimelech possessed the land. He inherited land in Bethlehem. Bethlehem literally means House of Bread. But the famine in their land means that the House of Bread was without bread! What an irony! What a reversal! There was a reason for it, though. The key is that those were the days of the judges. Everybody did whatever they wished.

"Eli," means "My God;" "Melech," means "King." So we have, "My God is King." I'm a child of the King! That's his name. His dad gave him that name because he wanted to honor God. This is where he comes from. He is starting very high. But we are going to see his walk. His walk is a descent.

2. What did Elimelech walk away from?

Elimelech went to live as a foreigner in the fields of Moab. Most English translations say "the land of Moab," but in Hebrew it is "the fields of Moab." That's very key because in Genesis 2 and 3 whenever it talks about outside of the Garden, it calls it "the fields."[73] So, in a way, this man is walking out of the Garden! He is walking out of the Land of Israel, out of the House of Bread, the house of provision. He's walking out of this and he's going down, leaving the Garden. His walk is revealing his heart.

---

[73]   Gen 2:5, 19–20; 3:1, 14, 18

Elimelech is also rejecting his inheritance in Israel. Later on in the book of Ruth, Boaz buys back Elimelech's land, which would've passed down to his two sons. In order for this man to leave Bethlehem he had to sell his property according to the stipulations of the Torah. The sell wasn't permanent, he "pawned" his property, so to speak, and walked away from it, from the land that was blessed, in a very fertile area of it.

His reason was the famine. There was a famine and he just got tired of waiting on God. They had a famine because they had a drought. They didn't have rain, and you can't survive in Israel without rain. So he waited. And waited. And he got tired of waiting on God. But God was waiting on him! Waiting on him to repent. But Elimelech was a very bitter man. Very frustrated and angry with God. I'll show you shortly how we know that.

This man goes to Moab and it says that he lived as a foreigner. Scripture talks about the foreigners, the widows and the orphans. It puts them in one category because they have one thing in common: they own no land. That's why God warns not to oppress them. He is their Defender because they are in this vulnerable category. But this man had a portion in the land that was blessed. He had a portion in the House of Bread and he walks away from it and goes to another country. He goes out of the Garden and lives without land.

We learned earlier that "the land" really is us. Elimelech takes his land, himself, and pawns it. He sells himself! He goes to the land of other gods, of people serving false gods, demons, and he has no land. He ends up working for others, and doesn't own himself anymore. He is in bondage. He gave up his freedom. He resisted repentance. God was knocking on his door and he was saying no. He was blaming God.

Ultimately, Elimelech chose not to depend on God. We know that for the following reason: The fields of Moab where he went didn't depend solely on the rain. The geography of Moab was such that they had rivers, and they were okay with droughts. At least that wouldn't affect them as much as it did Israel. The geographical and climatological conditions of Israel were such that they depended more on the rain. But in Moab you didn't need rain as much. You didn't need to depend on God. That's where Elimelech wanted to go.

Matthew 6 talks about seeking God's kingdom first and not worrying about what you would wear, eat and drink. The action of worrying is not just sitting and thinking. If you're really worried you get up and make sure you do something about it. You will make sure that you provide for yourself. That's why we have to kill worry early, or it will lead us to provide for ourselves, to take care of ourselves, not to depend on God. That's what Elimelech did. He went to a place where he didn't have to depend on God, where he could have a paycheck. He said, "I'm sick and tired of this. I just want security." And he left, revealing his heart.

Elimelech, in other words, reversed his redemption from Egypt! Think about it. He was freed from a land of foreign gods (Egypt), where he was a slave and where he owned no land. He received a good land, a blessed land, and a portion in probably the best part of that land. But he walked away from all of it and went back to working for somebody else as a servant. The primary Hebrew word for servant really means slave. He lost his land, lost his freedom and became a slave. He reversed his redemption from Egypt! Incredible!

Elimelech's Unfruitful Heart Revealed
- He walked out of the garden—from fruitfulness to cursed ground
- He rejected his inherited land in Israel
- He lived without land—sold himself
- He lived in the land of foreign gods, demons
- He refused to repent
- He chose not to have to depend on God for rain

3. Elimelech and Lot

Allow me to show you now what Elimelech and Lot have in common. Elimelech went to Moab. Who was Moab? Where did the Moabites come from? The Moabites were descendents of Lot, from one of the sons he had through his incestuous relationship with his daughters. Lot's descendents were the Moabites and the Ammonites. Elimelech is headed to that place. The word Moab means literally "From my father." And that's how Moab came to be. The boy Moab came from his mother's own father. That's why she named him that. Elimelech is a lot like Lot. How? Watch this:

First, Elimelech left the land of Israel. That's exactly what Lot did. Remember Lot and Abraham? Lot chose a place outside of the land of Canaan. Second, Lot went to a watered land. Lot chose Sodom and Gomorrah because it was the plains and you didn't have to depend on God, on rain. Lot's servants were fighting with Abraham's servants for the wells of water. And he needed water for his sheep. It was all about water. Third, both men went east. That has great significance. By going east you are going far from God's presence. Without them being aware of it, Lot and Elimelech's physical choices were prophetic of their spiritual choices, walking away from God. Forth, they lost their children. Didn't Lot loose his daughters? He sure did. He took them to Sodom and Gomorrah and look what happened. Same thing happened to Elimelech. His two children died. That's not a blessing from God!

	Lot	Elimelech
Left the Land of Israel	√	√
For watered land	√	√
Went east	√	√
Lost their children	√	√

4. Elimelech's journey of bitterness

Long before Elimelech took his wife and children east to Moab, he had already taken them on a spiritual journey away from God. Long before that. Let me show you. Verse 2:

> The name of the man was Elimelech, and the name of his wife, Naomi; and the names of his two sons were Mahlon and Chilion

The name Naomi means "Pleasant." Remember what she said when she came back to the land of Israel? She said, "I'm bitter." When she returned, her old girlfriends said to her: "Hey, Naomi, great to see you, it's been a long time." And she said: "Don't call me Naomi, don't call me 'Pleasant,' call me 'Mara.' 'Bitter.'"[74] Elimelech took his wife through a journey of bitterness.

Elimelech's first son was Mahlon. Do you know what that name means? "Sickly." And the other son? Chilion. That means "Destruction" or "Wasting Away," "Failing." How would you like to call your kids: "Hey, Sickly! Hey, Wasting Away! Bring your bikes! Time to eat!" How do you get there from "My God is King" and "Pleasant"? How do you get there? You get there by failing to repent.

Why did Elimelech name his kids that way? Because of what was happening around him. Due to the drought and the famine, his land was sick, and it was failing, everything around him. He couldn't take it. He was angry. He was upset. He was tired. He probably wished to change his own name too. He yelled at God saying, "I don't need this kind of a King! I AM NOT GOING TO GIVE MY CHILDREN THAT KIND OF A NAME! I'm going to call my child Sickly! How's that, God?" He was resisting God in his life.

---

[74] Ruth 1:19-20

It's very likely that some of you have gone or have been taken on a similar journey. Maybe you started as "Pleasant" and someone left you bitter. Someone took you on a journey you didn't want to go. You didn't know that would happen. All you saw was a future, a promise, some spirituality. And somebody took you out of the Garden! Maybe your father called you "Sickly," "Failing," or something. Maybe you are Elimelech! You've taken people on a journey of bitterness. Instead of allowing himself to just be broken, Elimelech chose to remain bitter. And in his bitterness, he made bitter his own wife and children.

CHAPTER SEVENTEEN

RAIN

Allow me to tell you a personal story. One time it rained in my city three days in a row. I was sick and tired of it! It's not supposed to rain that way where I live! If I wanted that much rain I would move elsewhere. Especially me, I grew up 30 minutes from the Caribbean. I just want good weather all the time!

I remember closing the bathroom door after that rain and thinking: Wait a minute, this door actually closed without any problem! Then I went to my front door and realized that the screen door which didn't use to close, would close fine now. My house had a bad foundation due to the dry ground. What had happened? The cracks were still on the walls, but everything seemed to have leveled. The rain fixed my foundation! Can you explain it any other way? The rain of God is fixing the foundation of my life!

> Is 45:8 Drip down, O heavens, from above, and let the clouds pour down righteousness; Let the earth open up and salvation bear fruit, and righteousness spring up with it.

The clouds drip and pour down, but it is not rain. What they drip and pour down is righteousness. This isn't talking about just regular rain, physical rain. It's talking about righteousness and it's going to fall on you and me. It says,

"Let the earth open up."

We are the earth, the ground. We are the soil, the good soil on which the good seed is planted. God sends the rain. It falls upon us, in our hearts. The earth needs to open up. It says,

"Let the earth open up and salvation bear fruit."

The earth has to open up and the work is going to be done by the rain. Salvation is going to spring up. It's going to give fruit. But the earth, you and I, need to open up. We do that through repentance, coming back to God.

Do you know what is the Hebrew word for Salvation here? It's Yeshua. This is Jesus' Hebrew name. Yeshua, Jesus, will bear fruit. Salvation will bear fruit. When you open up and He sends the rain, you will bear fruit. Righteousness will spring up with it.

You can't be righteous until you really love people. You may be religious. You may be a good person, but if it isn't love, it's not righteousness.

Salvation will bear fruit and the fruit is going to be righteousness, love! That love, righteousness, is the fruit that people will eat, because you are a tree. You are a vine.

When Jacob blessed Joseph, he said, "You are a vine. You are a fruitful vine growing on a wall."[75] And what did Joseph do for the whole world? He fed them. They ate from the bread that God gave him, in spite of his many sufferings. He fed people with his fruit, the fruit of his life. That's what God wants to do through all of us.

---

75   Gen 49:22

The names of Joseph's sons are Ephraim and Manasseh. Manasseh means to forget. Ephraim means fruitful. He forgot everything that happened to him, all the evil done to him. God healed him and he became fruitful. He was a vine. The vine gives grapes. What do you get from grapes? Wine. The Joy of the Spirit.

God wants to make you a joyous person. He wants to make you fruitful. He wants to give you bread. God wants you to be an amazing person!

The rain is the rain of righteousness. And righteousness is love. For someone to have a righteous walk he or she has to obey the Word of God. And the way you obey the Word of God is by loving God and loving people. Love is righteousness. You have acted righteously toward someone when you love him or her. Anything besides that is not righteous. Righteousness is love.

But you can't give what you don't have. You can't give what you haven't received. You can only love as you have received love. God's rain of righteousness, of love, heals your foundation, the foundations of your life. That's what Elimelech needed. He needed the rain. He thought he needed the rain for his physical land, but he didn't realize he needed the rain for his foundation, for his spiritual land, which was his heart. He lived that way, and he died that way. His children died that way too. They died cursed. His two sons died without children, a curse in the Torah. And thus Elimelech's name would never be remembered. His descendants will be no more. They died unfruitful. What a sobering thought!

Maybe you need to have God loosen the grip of bitterness. If it isn't you who have taken someone on a journey of bitterness, maybe you've been taken on a journey of bitterness, and you live with the consequences of someone bitter. You need to experience God's goodness, so you can believe again and trust. Some people are like Naomi, others are like her sons, and some are like Elimelech. Some have been hurt as a wife or by a wife. Some have been hurt as a child or by a child. And some are Elimelech, whether man or woman.

Many times the way to achieve repentance is to forgive. If you want lasting repentance in your life, go a little deeper and see who you may need to forgive. It may be painful, but it'll heal you. You will find areas that are going to unlock and you will experience God's forgiveness. You will be healed! You will be free. When this happens you will see the water coming down to your life in areas that were rocky, in areas that were filled with thorns and thistles. In areas that are dead. In unfruitful hearts.

CHAPTER EIGHTEEN

HEALING AND FREEDOM

Let's look now at the names Elimelech gave his children, Sickly and Destruction. Let's consider first Sickly, Mahlon. The word highlighted in each of the following verses represents the Hebrew word related to the name Mahlon.

> Ex 15:26 And He said, "If you will give earnest heed to the voice of the LORD your God, and do what is right in His sight, and give ear to His commandments, and keep all His statutes, I will put none of the **diseases** on you which I have put on the Egyptians; for I, the LORD, am your healer.[76]

Why did those diseases come to Egypt? Because they hardened their hearts toward God. They didn't repent. Just like Elimelech.

> Ex 23:25 But you shall serve the LORD your God, and He will bless your bread and your water; and I will remove **sickness** from your midst.

---

[76] The highlighted portions of the verses in this chapter have been added for emphasis.

The Holy Spirit was talking to Elimelech: "I want to bless your bread. I want to bless you Elimelech, you who live in the House of Bread. I want to bless your water. You have no water. I can solve that. I can change your child's name. You and your land would be sickly no more."

> Is 17:11 In the day that you plant it you carefully fence it in, and in the morning you bring your seed to blossom; but the harvest will be a heap in a day of **sickliness** and incurable pain.

Again, here is a picture of a man who has a crop, a harvest, but it becomes nothing because the condition of his heart spills out into the physical world. There's no fruitfulness in him. Jesus said, "Whoever does not have, even what he has shall be taken away from him."[77]

> Is 53:4 Surely our **griefs** He Himself bore

Here are some solutions. The Hebrew word translated "griefs" is the same root word for sickly. And Matthew quotes that and says, in reference to Jesus going out and healing people,

> Matt 8:17 This was to fulfill what was spoken through Isaiah the prophet: "HE HIMSELF TOOK OUR INFIRMITIES AND CARRIED AWAY OUR DISEASES."

Jesus had just healed Peter's mother-in-law and healed many people and cast out many demons.

> 1 Peter 2:24 And He Himself bore our sins in His body on the cross, so that we might die to sin and

---

[77] Matt 13:12

live to righteousness; for by His wounds you were healed.

In Jesus' death we find healing. That applies to both, spiritual and physical healing. Matthew applied it to physical healing, and Peter applies it to spiritual healing, to the healing of our souls. We have both. We have to experience healing in order to experience freedom. You cannot be free unless you are healed. Elimelech's two sons' names reveal this. One of them, Sickly, needs healing, and the other one needs freedom from curses.

Let's consider now verses about the other son, Destruction, Chilion. As before, the word highlighted in each of the following verses represents the Hebrew word related to the name Chilion.

> Josh 24:20 If you forsake the LORD and serve foreign gods, then He will turn and do you harm and **consume** you after He has done good to you.

> Lam 4:11 The LORD has accomplished His wrath, He has poured out His fierce anger; and He has kindled a fire in Zion which has **consumed** its foundations.

Elimelech's foundations were consumed, destroyed. When he named his son Destruction he was prophesying about himself. He didn't even know it! It was his foundations that were destroyed. The book of Lamentation is talking about the foundations of the Temple. But we are the temple. How are your foundations? How can we solve that? How can we find healing and freedom?

> Job 33:21 His flesh **wastes away** from sight, and his bones which were not seen stick out.

> Psa 90:9 For all our days have declined in Your fury; we have **finished** our years like a sigh.

Psa 102:3 For my days have been **consumed** in smoke, and my bones have been scorched like a hearth.

Time goes by, with no purpose. Years go by, my life ends and I have nothing to show for it. That's Elimelech.

Jer 5:10 Go up through her vine rows and destroy, but do not execute a complete **destruction**; strip away her branches, for they are not the LORD'S. God in His compassion still leaves some remnant seeking repentance.

Jer 46:28 O Jacob My servant, do not fear," declares the LORD, "For I am with you. For I will **make a full end** of all the nations where I have driven you, yet I will not **make a full end** of you; but I will correct you properly and by no means leave you unpunished."

We saw healing because the other son was Sickly, and God can heal. Jesus brings physical and spiritual healing. That's the first son. The second son speaks of freedom. Jeremiah says here, "For I am with you. For I will make a full end of all the nations where I have driven you . . ." God sent Israel to Babylon, to captivity, as punishment. But He said, "I'm coming now to judge them, just like I came and judged the Egyptians. And I will bring complete destruction to them, but I will bring you out." Are you in captivity? Are you in a foreign "land" like Elimelech was? Has God sent you there? Have your sins taken you there? God is going to bring you back. He wants to heal you, and then He will bring punishment over your enemies. Because of the judgment that took place at the cross you can be free. Healing and deliverance. Elimelech's sons. God was speaking to him. "Do you want to name your children that? I can reverse that!"

> Jer 46:28 "For I will make a full end of all the
> nations where I have driven you, yet I will not make
> a full end of you; but I will correct you properly and
> by no means leave you unpunished."

In that correction there's freedom. God takes care of the enemy.

> Ezek 20:17 Yet My eye spared them rather
> than destroying them, and I did not cause their
> **annihilation** in the wilderness. I'm seeking for
> some who are going to repent, and I'm going to
> heal them and bring them back.

Allow me now to quote a verse that was very surprising to me as I found out how it relates to all this.

> John 19:30 Therefore when Jesus had received the
> sour wine, He said, "It is finished!"

The Greek word translated "finished" is used in the Greek Old Testament, the Septuagint, to translate the Hebrew word related to Elimelech's son Chilion. Jesus took everything upon Himself to the end, and because He did that then you can walk away free. His judgment over our enemies was a total destruction! It has been finished! They have been destroyed! Because Jesus' work is done, your bondage is done, your destruction is stopped!

What about you and me now? There's hope! There's healing! There's freedom! Be still, and see the salvation that the Lord will perform. You won't have to fight. The time is coming soon when you will see the waters come down on Pharaoh's demons that oppress you and you will see your enemies no more. You will be free! You will overcome your unfruitful heart!

What you and I need is rain: a revelation of God's love by His Spirit for healing. We need to hear and to see God loving us at the moment of our wounding. We need to return to the land of rain and fruitfulness. Watch God fill your previously unfruitful heart with the fruit of life, of love. Love toward God and people. You will overcome your unfruitful heart!

CONCLUSION

Not many Bible stories have a good ending, but this one does. Naomi's journey of bitterness ends with her returning, both physically and spiritually, to the House of Bread, Bethlehem.

Ruth, on the other hand, was urged by Naomi to stay in Moab.

> Ruth 1:8-9 And Naomi said to her two daughters-in-law, "Go, return each of you to her mother's house. May the LORD deal kindly with you as you have dealt with the dead and with me. "May the LORD grant that you may find rest, each in the house of her husband."

Orpah, Naomi's other daughter-in-law, chose to not leave the fields of Moab but to remain outside the House of Bread, returning to her mother's house in order to find a husband. The reality is that Orpah's decision was also a spiritual one.

> Ruth 1:15 Then she said, "Behold, your sister-in-law has gone back to her people and her gods; return after your sister-in-law."

Ruth, however, responded with her now famous words.

> Ruth 1:16-17 But Ruth said, "Do not urge me to leave you or turn back from following you; for where

you go, I will go, and where you lodge, I will lodge. Your people shall be my people, and your God, my God. "Where you die, I will die, and there I will be buried. Thus may the LORD do to me, and worse, if anything but death parts you and me."

By choosing a fruitful mother, Ruth also received a fruitful husband. Notice what was different about her.

> Ruth 1:18-19 When she [Naomi] saw that she [Ruth] was determined to go with her, she said no more to her. So they both went until they came to Bethlehem.

Ruth was "determined to go" with Naomi. Then they both "went" until they came to the House of Bread. The Hebrew word translated "determined" means to be strong. The verb is reflexive, indicating that Ruth was both the one doing the action and the recipient of it. In other words, she strengthened herself in God. She "rallied herself"[78] and defied her fears. For what reason did she strengthened herself? "To go." The word "go" is again the normal word for the spiritual walk of the believer. This is also the same word translated "went" in verse 19. Ruth's spiritual walk led her to the House of Bread.

When Ruth and Naomi came to the House of Bread they found the opposite of Elimelech in more than one way.

> Ruth 1:22 So Naomi returned, and with her Ruth the Moabitess, her daughter-in-law, who returned from the land of Moab. And they came to Bethlehem at the beginning of barley harvest.

---

[78] NIDOTTE, s.v. "ametz" 2:429.

Ruth 2:1 Now Naomi had a kinsman of her husband, a man of great wealth, of the family of Elimelech, whose name was Boaz.

Obviously, Boaz is the opposite of Elimelech. However, the details of Scripture point us to deeper realities not so obvious on the surface.

Exodus

Ruth and Naomi returned to Israel at the beginning of the barley harvest. This harvest begins two days after Passover every year. This means that the Exodus from Egypt was in the mind of everyone, and was the spiritual atmosphere in which the Spirit of God was moving during those days. Was Naomi aware of this as she was returning back to Israel? Absolutely! How can I be so sure? Notice what she said when she returned:

> Ruth 1:19-21 So they both went until they came to Bethlehem. And when they had come to Bethlehem, all the city was stirred because of them, and the women said, "Is this Naomi?" She said to them, "Do not call me Naomi; call me Mara, for the Almighty has dealt very bitterly with me. "I went out full, but the LORD has brought me back empty. Why do you call me Naomi, since the LORD has witnessed against me and the Almighty has afflicted me?"

One of the main features of the Passover is the bitter herbs that Israel should eat along with the lamb, in order to remember the bitter oppression of their bondage in Egypt. Naomi arrived in Israel right after the Passover, which means she had her Passover while still in Moab. There, that Passover night, no doubt the Lord sealed her experience of repentance and return speaking to her about her journey of bitterness. She had gone along with Elimelech in reversing their exodus from Egypt. They had sold their land, their soul, and like Lot they sought watered land in their drought. But instead she found bitterness in their iniquity. She found herself in bondage and needed God to once again give her healing and freedom. As Naomi and Ruth walked in repentance back to the House of Bread, God gave them a new exodus.

Boaz and Elimelech turn the story of the prodigal son and his brother upside down. Although Elimelech was the older of the two, and although he was the one bitter in his heart against God, he was the one who left for a foreign country and threw away his life prostituting himself to other gods. Conversely, Boaz was the younger of the two and never left, nonetheless he wasn't bitter against God.

Boaz treated his servants with kindness, which is a reflection of a heart of compassion and not of oppression. Boaz was a son, not a slave and an oppressor, and he treated God's children as sons. He had challenges, however. He was unmarried. God had not provided a wife for him yet. But Boaz didn't agree with Satan's lies and accusations that surely came against God as a bad Father and Provider. Boaz didn't agree with Satan to feel pity for himself, or to feel like a failure, a reject, maybe even a man not attractive enough. Instead, Boaz experienced a fruitful life, with rain and crops. Boaz was waiting on God's promise of translating the blessing of fruitfulness into a family life as well.

What was Boaz's spiritual heritage? Look who his parents were:

> Matt 1:5 Salmon was the father of Boaz by Rahab,
> Boaz was the father of Obed by Ruth.

Boaz's mother was none other than Rahab, the former prostitute who hid the spies and was granted protection from death as Israel conquered Jericho. His father was the amazing man who went to Jericho as a spy with the faith of the former spies Joshua and Caleb. Salmon did not oppress Rahab by reminding her what she had been and how undeserving she was of God. By raising Boaz, a fruitful son, full of compassion and faith, we see the deep healing and freedom that Salmon and Rahab experienced.

YOU

God wants to give you a story like Naomi's. He wants to give you a story of healing and freedom, a story of returning to the House of Bread in repentance from living in the land of self-reliance. If you have reversed your exodus and find yourself under Pharaoh's hand in bondage, God has paid the price to set you free. Jesus' death for you defeated your enemy forever. That victory brings you healing and freedom, compassion and redemption.

God wants to give you a story like Ruth's. God wants to give you a fruitful mother like He gave Ruth, a mother that has repented and is walking toward fruitfulness. A "mother" is the person that teaches you.

> Gal 4:19 My children, with whom I am again in labor until Christ is formed in you.

Whoever teaches you will give you what he or she has. Paul was "in labor." That's a motherly picture. He was the spiritual "mother," and God Himself the Father. Orpah returned to her mother's house, to her gods. Ruth clung to Naomi, to Naomi's God. One found further bondage, the other found fruitfulness, a fruitful husband. Find a compassionate teacher who ministers healing and freedom, not bondage and affliction. Being a son of God and not a slave, and having a "mother," a compassionate teacher, leads you to your Husband, Jesus, the one who makes you fruitful through healing and freedom.

God wants to give you a story like Boaz's. He delivered Boaz from the generational iniquities and curses of his ancestors, and made him a fruitful man. Not only did God delivered him from his mother's iniquities, He also delivered him from his father's heritage of wilderness rebellion and wandering. God made him a man who ministered compassion and acceptance to his peers and his own wife. He ministered dignity to men and women alike. He defended the cause of the poor (Ruth and Naomi), the widows (Naomi) and the foreigner (Ruth). Therefore, God gladly gave him rain and crops: Barley, wheat, grapes and olives. In other words, God gave him bread, joy and sanctification. Boaz's storehouses were full of these products for him to eat and to feed others.

May God bless you too with freedom to be fruitful!